WHY YOU MIGHT WANT TO READ

GRACE ON TAP

Grace. It can be one of the most misunderstood, misrepresented concepts in Christianity. People everywhere attempt to grasp its reality, discover its potential, and tap into its power. But too often, we miss the truth of what it truly is. In this powerful and perspective-changing book, my good friend Eric Dykstra uncovers the reality of grace in our lives. And as he shows readers just what grace is and what it isn't, he reveals its transformational power to change everything in our lives!

Ed Young
Pastor, Fellowship Church
Author, *Outrageous, Contagious Joy*

Grace on Tap *helped me see how thorough salvation is for all of us. I have taught the New Testament verse by verse for over 35 years, but reading this book opened my eyes even more. I'll highly recommend it to every member of St. James Church and anyone else who will listen to me! Thank you, Eric!*

Ted Haggard
Pastor, St. James Church, Colorado Springs, CO

In **Grace On Tap***, Eric Dykstra simply yet brilliantly breaks down some of the biggest misunderstandings and myths about the true message of the cross. Whether you've been a Christian for 50 years or are simply exploring faith, this book will lead you to a deeper understanding of the Christian message and the life God intends for all of us!*

Bil Cornelius
Founding Pastor, Bay Area Fellowship, and best-selling author of
I Dare You to Change and *Today is the Day*

The grace of God is a truth so rich and deep that you can mine its depths all of your life and never reach the bottom, yet it's available to you everyday, free, "on tap"! Get ready to see Jesus and your life with fresh eyes of grace!

Brad White
Pastor, LifePoint Church, Tampa, Florida

Eric Dykstra

Published by Crossing Church Publishing
829 School Street
Elk River, Minnesota 55330

www.crossing-church.com

Some names in stories have been changed to protect privacy.

ISBN 978-0-9896828-0-0

To my amazing children, Braden, Holland, and Aidan:

I dedicate this book to you, prayerfully believing that the grace of God will hit you earlier than it hit me.

I want you to go further with God than your mom and I ever have. I declare in faith that if your foundation is grace and not law, you will do greater things. You will make better choices, influence more people, and advance the kingdom of Jesus further than I can even dream.

Grace is the key to a life of blessing for you.

Hold on to grace above all else.

I am so excited to see what God is going to do next with you.

- Dad

TABLE OF CONTENTS

Karli Phelps: Thank you for your red pen and the wisdom with which you use it. (I almost said, "...the wisdom you use it with".)

Renee Huisinga and Maggie DeHaven: Thank you for doing research on self-publishing. You know how I feel about details.

Jacob Wernersbach: Thank you for designing the website and helping to get the word out.

Whitney Berre: Thank you for, well, everything. Seriously, you're good at everything. Our life changed when you entered it.

And finally, to the incredible staff and people of The Crossing Church: Thank you for giving me grace as I transitioned from a law-based faith to a grace-based faith. Thank you for sticking with me as I began to explore grace and haltingly began to teach it. Thank you for letting it become part of who we are at The Crossing. I will forever be grateful to God for you. I love you all.

Grace and peace to you through Christ Jesus.

FOREWORD

I am so excited about the journey you're about to begin through the pages of this book. Your beliefs will be challenged, your spirit encouraged, your faith stirred, and you will see, understand and be in awe of the gift God has given you.

My friend Eric has discovered something very simple yet profound—that the gospel is GOOD NEWS. Of course we all would agree with that statement in theory, because that is what the word "gospel" means. But practically speaking it's a different story for way too many of God's children. Most are worn out, broken down, tired, and burned out. And many more have called it quits saying that they've "tried" Christianity.

For many years I strived, worked, and climbed trying to be accepted and qualified in God's eyes. This made me miserable as my entire life was focused around me and the sins I committed or was about to commit. I lived sin-focused instead of Savior-focused.

I quietly replaced my Savior with a system, a person with a program, and a relationship with a religion. What happened was that it created fear, insecurity, exhaustion, anger, condemnation, guilt, and shame in me. And none of this was placed on me by God, but by the religion I was creating myself.

In my mind, I felt as though God was never satisfied with me. I felt like I always had to work hard to please Him because He was a God who was cranky, fickle and ready to squish the fun and life out of me every time I messed up. Every day was like walking on eggshells on a balance beam, as I would wait to see if God was happy with me or angry with me. It was schizophrenic Christianity at its worst.

Not only was I believing that the gospel was "bad news" that revolved around me, but as a pastor, I was teaching people

INTRODUCTION
PAYING FOR WHAT WAS FREE
(A simple illustration for making sense of Grace on Tap.)

In order to understand this book, you must first hear about an experience that profoundly changed my life.

Several months ago, Kelly and me were invited to a wedding. The wedding was beautiful, and we were having a great time with our friends at the reception. Kelly asked if I would go up to the bar and get a couple of drinks for us. So, up to the bar I went. I ordered two glasses of Merlot for Kelly and I and a kiddie cocktail for our youngest son, Aidan. The bill came to $13. I threw in $2 for a tip and returned to our table with the drinks.

As I sat down, I handed my daughter some cash. Kelly said, "What are you doing?"

"Giving Holland some cash for a drink."

Kelly gave me the weirdest look. "Honey, it's an open bar!"

"Well, they charged me!" I shot back.

"Eric, this wedding has an open bar! Why on earth did they charge you?!"

"I don't know, but they did," I insisted, a bit defensively.

"OK, the bar is right over there!" she said, pointing to the far corner of the room. "Where did you go for the drinks?"

Suddenly I felt kind of dumb. "In the lobby." Realization began to strike.

I had gone to the cash bar in the lobby, when the father of the bride had already paid for an open bar in the reception hall! I had

PART 1: THE THEOLOGY OF GRACE

CHAPTER 1

THE VERSE THAT CHANGED MY LIFE FOREVER

"If you remove grace out of the gospel, the gospel is gone."
- C. H. Spurgeon

Many people believe there are two "works of grace" in a person's life. One, when they "get saved". Two, when they are "baptized" in the Spirit and they speak in tongues or get fresh revelation of who God is. I don't know if that is true or not. But it is true *for me*.

I have been *"born again"* twice.

I asked Jesus into my life at age seventeen. I was in New York state at a Bible camp, and I got down on my knees at a campfire and I asked Jesus Christ to forgive my sins and lead my life. And He did! He moved into my life, forgave me of my past, and began to transform me. My friends began asking me why I was so different. I even went off to a Bible college to enter a life of full-time ministry. I was a changed man.

But then a strange thing happened. My well-intentioned teachers, pastors, and churches taught me (unintentionally) that after you come to Jesus for forgiveness, you must prove you really love Jesus by being obedient to Him!

Or, said another way:

We get righteousness at the cross, but we stay righteous by working for it.

And so, I began to work really hard at obeying Jesus. I read my Bible every day. I memorized Scripture. I prayed. I served in my church. I witnessed to my friends. I worked hard at fighting temptation. I tried to be a "man of holiness". I started a church. I preached the gospel. I led people to Jesus. I tithed. I gave sacrificially. I...

Do you see all the I's in that paragraph? I was trying to achieve my own righteousness. I was going to be a sold-out Christian. Except it never worked, and I always felt like a failure. No matter how much I did, I felt like it was never enough. I never served enough, gave enough, preached enough, loved enough, and prayed enough. I never felt righteous, no matter how hard I tried. And the more I went to church or read the Bible, the more I just felt like a failure; because I could never live up to the standard of perfection in the Bible.

That is until Jesus met me with a second work of grace. One day while on a vacation from ministry, I stumbled across 2 Corinthians 5:21.

The more I read this verse and studied its implications, the more it messed me up. The more it messed me up, the more I would cry and shake and tremble before God. I spent an entire month immersed in the study of this verse. At the end of one month, I was a totally different human being. I knew I measured up. I knew I wasn't a failure. I knew I was strong enough. Had faith enough. I was a totally different person. Jesus had met me; He had done a second work of grace in me. My church said I was different. My staff said I was different. My wife and kids said I was different.

The grace of God had hit me, and I was born again. Again.

Here is the verse that messed me up forever:

2 Corinthians 5:21 God made him who had no sin to be sin for us, so that in him we might become the righteousness of God.

Let me break this verse down for you. Here is the first half:

2 Corinthians 5:21 God made him who had no sin to be sin for us...

Jesus BECAME your sin at the cross. He didn't just remove your sin; He BECAME your sin! When you are looking at the cross, you are seeing Jesus AS you! Every lie, every dirty thought, every bad attitude, bad word, and bad deed you ever did - He became it! And after BECOMING your sin, He then died in your place.

Jesus died in your place, paying the price for all your sin and shame. He took the punishment that was meant for you.

Think about that: If Jesus took the punishment for you, there is NO punishment for you - EVER! Jesus took it. If Jesus became your sin, God is not ever going to give you a beat down for your sin, because Jesus took your beat down. If Jesus died in your place, God is not mad at you, because He got mad at Jesus. God can be proud of you!

He BECAME your sin. Your price has been totally paid forever! That is beautiful news of grace. But the verse is not done yet, it gets even better.

The second part of 2 Corinthians 5:21 says ...*so that in him we might* *become* *the righteousness of God.*

Do you see that?

Jesus became your sin in the first part of the verse, but YOU became the righteousness of God in the second. A divine exchange took place at the cross. Jesus became sin; you became righteous!

Now, the word "righteous" is a big word that we don't use much anymore, so let me define it for you.

"Righteous" means, "not guilty, entirely pleasing to God".

Whoa! Do you know what means? At the cross, that is what YOU BECAME! You became "not guilty, entirely pleasing to God".

Say that out loud 3 times:

I am NOT GUILTY. I am ENTIRELY PLEASING TO GOD!

This is the gift Jesus paid to give you at the cross!

You don't have to work to be righteous. You are righteous. Right now. As you are.

You don't have to try to be more like Jesus. You are already like Jesus.

You don't have to try to be a better person. You are a totally different person. You ARE entirely pleasing to God.
That is the good news of the gospel.

I didn't understand this for years. I spent most of my life as a Christian working, trying to be "pleasing to God" so that God might hopefully say to me someday, *"Well done, good and faithful servant!" -Matthew 25:23*

When 2 Corinthians 5:21 washed over me, suddenly it hit me:

Jesus was GOOD, and Jesus was FAITHFUL, and Jesus was a SERVANT, and He gave me HIS righteousness at the cross. It was His gift to me! So, I don't have to work to be good or faithful or a servant. I AM ALREADY A GOOD AND FAITHFUL SERVANT because of Jesus.

So the only thing I will ever hear from God is, "WELL DONE, GOOD AND FAITHFUL SERVANT!" because I am the righteousness of God in Christ Jesus.

And the same is true for you. God is proud of you. You are not a failure. You measure up. Why? Because Jesus gave you His righteousness at the cross.

That is what Grace is! Not only were you forgiven, but you were also made righteous!

For you who are working your brains out trying to please God but always feel like a failure (I have been there; I feel your pain) - God is already proud of you.

For those of you living under a burden of guilt thinking if *only* you could sin less (I know; I lived for years in guilt) - You are a saint, not a sinner, in God's eyes.

For those of you that are depressed at the thought of walking into heaven worried about how God views you, be glad. You will hear, "WELL DONE GOOD AND FAITHFUL SERVANT!" BECAUSE OF JESUS!

It seems like Christians talk a lot about grace. We sing "Amazing Grace", and we say grace before meals, but we don't really know what grace is. At least I didn't. Maybe I am the only one out there who didn't get it, but I doubt it.

I grew up Baptist. Not Southern Baptist. Another Association of Just Plain Baptists. We were so strict that we thought Southern Baptists were going to hell (no, I'm not joking).

Everything about our faith was a 'thou shalt not'. Don't drink, dance, play cards, listen to music with drumbeats, go to movies (God must have been against art), swear, or have any friends that do any of the aforementioned. You also could not be a member unless you signed a covenant and vowed you would not do any of these things.

By the time I was 15 I was pretty well burned out on the whole rules thing and had moved on to full-on rebellion against God and my parents. Well, not completely full on. I went to church because my parents made me, but I lived with a heart that resented God, and it played out in near-hatred toward my dad and his rules.

Even though it was a rules-driven church, I would still hear preachers talk about grace. Many times, they would give us this acrostic: God's Riches At Christ's Expense.

It was taught like this: Jesus died on the cross to give you forgiveness of all your sins. The riches of grace is forgiveness, and the expense of grace was the cross. So, come to Christ and He will forgive you!

This is true! I believe this. Grace does mean forgiveness, but grace is so much richer than forgiveness! Jesus didn't just die to forgive me of my sin. He died so I could be clothed in His righteousness. He died so I could live every day, "not guilty, entirely pleasing to God."

Because of the cross, when God looks at us He sees the goodness of His Son! It is not that God is just benevolently forgiving you of your evil. He is applauding you and He is proud of you because all of Christ's good works were applied to you.

That is what Grace is. It is forgiveness of sin, but also CREDIT for Christ's goodness.

Let me give you several Scriptures on this, starting with the book of Zechariah. Let's read through the story of the high priest, Jeshua, and his encounter with God.

Zechariah 3:1-4 Then the angel showed me Jeshua the high priest standing before the angel of the LORD. Satan was there at the angel's right hand, accusing Jeshua of many things. (NLT)

According to this, Satan's role in the world is to accuse you before God of all the things that you do wrong. He is the accuser. His name actually means this!

He stands over you daily and whispers... "God saw how you treated your wife yesterday. You are so worthless. I can't believe you said that to her. You don't even deserve to be called a Christian. God is embarrassed by you. He knows what you think about when no one else is around. He knows all the sin that is really in your heart."

Satan throws these kinds of accusations at us all day, every day and, if we listen to them, we feel like a worthless piece of trash. We live guilt-ridden, depressed, and embarrassed.

But notice what God replies to Satan:

Zechariah 3:2 And the LORD said to Satan, "I, the LORD, reject your accusations, Satan. Yes, the LORD, who has chosen Jerusalem, rebukes you. This man is like a burning stick that has been snatched from a fire." (NLT)

"No Satan, I will not listen to this garbage about how my child does not measure up! I reject these accusations! I chose him! I snatched him from the path of death and hell, and have chosen him as my own!" That is the GOOD NEWS OF GRACE!

God rejects all of the accusations that Satan speaks over your life. God rejects all of the accusations that others speak over your life as well. When your wife, your boss, your co-workers, or your classmates accuse you and condemn you – God rejects those accusations even if they are true!

See, Jesus died to change the truth about you. He died so the truth is that you are not a sinner, even though you sinned. Now you are a saint in God's eyes. Complete, good, entirely pleasing to God.

If you are in Christ, God rejects all condemning voices about you!

Jeshua's clothing was filthy as he stood there before the angel. So the angel said to the others standing there, *"Take off his filthy clothes."* And turning to Jeshua he said, *"See, I have*

Growing up super-strict Baptist I saw the opposite of grace. One time a man came to church without a suit on. The usher approached him and whispered in his ear, "You can't come to a service without a sport coat. We have one we can loan you from our lobby." Then the man was escorted to the lobby and returned to his seat wearing a cheap, polyester sport jacket.

We were a church clothed in rules, not grace! This is the opposite of grace; this is LAW!

Where grace removes our striving and regulations and hoops, the law adds to them. The law in scripture is a list of rules we must follow to be liked and blessed by God.

The Ten Commandments in the Old Testament were God's rules given to Moses so the children of Israel could be liked and blessed by God. If they obeyed them, they were blessed. If they disobeyed, they were cursed.

Most Christians take The Ten Commandments and try to live by them and then add their own, extra, even more legalistic spin. Don't be around gay people because their gayness might rub off on you. Don't smoke because you are breathing in hellfire. Don't watch 'R' rated movies because you will go out and shoot people, swear and snort coke. Don't have sex standing up because it leads to dancing. The list just goes on and on and on.

We add rules because we think it will help us be more like Jesus. The problem is, rules don't make us more like Jesus. Rules are the OPPOSITE of grace AND GRACE IS WHO JESUS IS!

Law says, "I must obey to be blessed."

Grace says, "Jesus obeyed, so I am blessed no matter what!"

Religions are always built around laws. They all tell you what you have to do so that God will like you and bless you. Grace is the only thing that separates Christianity from other religions.

Let me help you understand grace and law with some symbols: letters, ladders, and scales:

Letters:
D-O! Religion, even for most Christians, is spelled DO. Give more, go more, serve more, be more, act more, speak more, listen more, read more, even love more. Religion is always spelled D-O! DO DO DO! Then God will like you and bless you! The problem with this is that you never feel like you did enough.

It is a giant black hole that you can never fill. And pretty soon your life is filled with doo-doo and it just stinks.

Ladders:
Religion tells you, "If you can just climb up this achievement ladder, you can be where God is. God likes the obedient ones and curses the disobedient ones, so CLIMB, MONKEY, CLIMB!" The problem is there is always one more rung to climb, one more deed to do, one more Bible verse to read, one more dollar to give. It is exhausting and frustrating and depressing. And pretty soon you start to feel like a monkey climbing a ladder.

Scales:
Religion says, "If my good deeds outweigh my bad deeds, God will be proud of me and accept me and love me." The only problem is, my good deeds never seem like enough. There is always the question in the back of your mind; "Did I do enough to balance out the bad? I hope so. I better do a little more just to make sure!" But the bad never seems to go away. My past always haunts me. It is always right there accusing me. So I live hoping, but never knowing, that my good outweighs my bad. Scales always make me feel fat and lousy.

Here's what is really cool: the symbol of Christianity. It is not the letters D-O, and it is not ladders or scales. The symbol of Christianity is a cross.

Jesus DID all the work for me to get blessed at the cross. Religion is spelled D-O; a relationship with Christ is spelled D-O-N-E! Jesus did all the work so I could be forgiven and entirely pleasing to God! All is grace!

Jesus climbed the ladder for me with His life and death on the cross. He was perfect and righteous, and then He gave me credit for His perfection and righteousness at the cross. The ladder has been climbed, and I was given an elevator to the top floor! I am the righteousness of God in Christ Jesus, so I get the penthouse of heaven! All is grace!

Jesus took the evil of my life off my scale, and put His goodness on the scale at the cross. If I am weighed and measured by God, all He sees is Christ's righteousness! So I am not fat with sin, I am well pleasing to God. All is grace!

This is the core of the gospel message. All is grace! No matter what you heard from the TV preachers, no matter what your Christian radio station said, no matter what was chiseled in stone 4,000 years ago. You were given grace, which means you don't have to achieve favor; you have favor.

Let me say it again: you don't have to achieve favor; you have favor. God just wants to bless you, be good to you, and is proud of you. You were given these gifts freely at the cross!

If you're reading this, you are likely a religious person or Christian. What brought you to Christ? The rules of Christianity, or what you heard about His grace?

I have never met anyone who came to Christ because of rules! "Hey, I'd like a list of rules I have to achieve. That sounds fun! I'll believe in God for that." No. We came to Christ because of Christ's grace and the hope of a better life. If you didn't come to Jesus to get some rules, why do you think that following rules is the way to grow in your faith?

Many churches (and ours has been guilty of this) draw seekers with the message of grace and the hope of life "to the full", but the minute they cross the line of faith, we show them the list of expectations so they'll try to create that life through their own efforts. The disservice we do them is beyond wrong. And we can't figure out why once-enthusiastic new believers walk right out the back door of the church, never to be seen again.

If you try to achieve your faith through a list after starting out in grace, you will fail or QUIT! This is why Paul said, *"**Are you so foolish? After beginning with the Spirit, are you now trying to attain your goal by human effort?**" -Galatians 3:3*

The opposite of grace is human effort. Leave your do-do behind and come back to Jesus and His finished work.

CHAPTER 4

THE FIRE HOSE OF LAW AND GRACE

"Faith is a living, daring confidence in God's grace, so sure and certain that a man could stake his life on it a thousand times."
- Martin Luther

Now I know you may not be convinced yet. I needed it beat into my head before I saw it, so I am going to help you drink from a fire hose of Scripture for a few minutes. My hope is that this law and grace thing starts to sink in for you, too.

Don't go to sleep for this chapter. Stay focused. It's like those 3D posters. Squint, look from different angles, throw your eyes out of focus (OK, maybe that won't help), but take your time and study these verses until they are clear to you. They will transform your whole life!

This is so important, I want to pray for you before I start this section.

Jesus Christ, the great grace-bringer, I ask that by Your name and by Your blood, You would break down the wall of religion, pride, desire to achieve, and self-righteousness and help every person reading this book to see the TRUTH OF YOUR GRACE! I ask for You to help people have an open mind to the powerful TRUTH OF GRACE. I ask for you to loose supernatural insight and focus as they read these verses. And I ask that GRACE would transform their souls, hearts, minds, and lives forever. In the name of Jesus Christ, AMEN.

Ok, now you can read these verse on law and grace. I will make some comments after each verse. But if you disagree with me, go read the whole passage in context. I am not crazy! (Well, yes I am. But in a good, grace-filled way.)

Galatians 2:21 I do not set aside the grace of God, for if righteousness could be gained through the law, Christ died for nothing!

What are we to never set aside? Grace! Goodness cannot be found in the law.

Think of the law like a rigged carnival game in which God said, "You will be righteous if you can throw the ring on the bottles." But no matter how many times we throw the ring, we always fail! How about we stop playing the ring game? Let's just trust that Jesus already played this game perfectly and that His scorecard was given to us. NOW WE GET THE STUFFED TEDDY BEAR!

Romans 3:20 ...through the law we become conscious of sin.

What does the law do? Makes us sin-conscious.

Think of the law like a mirror. When you look in a mirror, what do you notice? All your flaws! My hair is out of place. There's a big zit. I have a booger in my right nostril. A mirror shows us our flaws. That is also what the law does. When you hold the law up, it shows you all your faults and failures. When you hear about the Ten Commandments - thou shalt not lie or cheat or steal or commit adultery - what do you think about? You think of all the moments in your life when you totally jacked those rules up! The law reveals our flaws.

What many pastors and church leaders do is preach these rules to you so that you will change. But no matter how much you preach the law IT CAN'T CHANGE YOU! It just reveals your flaws.

If you take a mirror and scrub it on your face it will not clean you, but it might cut you! So why are churches scrubbing the law on your face like it will help you? It can't help you; it only cuts you!

[Side note: I am not saying the law is bad. It isn't bad. It just isn't the solution to your sin problem any more than a mirror is a solution to your facial flaws!]

Romans 2:15 They demonstrate that God's law is written in their hearts... (NLT)

Where is the law written? On our hearts. So why do I need to teach the law to you? You already know how guilty you are! It is written on your heart!

My youngest son, Aidan, is eleven. One night a few weeks back, after the lights were out and we were in bed, he came into our room and said, "DAD!" First of all, he scared the crap out of me, but secondly I noticed he was crying.

"What is it, Aidan?"

"I feel bad, Dad."

"Why?"

"I had a bad thought!"

"You had a bad thought. When was that?"

"I dunno, when I was like nine!"

My youngest son was standing in my room guilt-ridden for a bad thought he had when he was nine! Why? Because the law is written on our hearts! We already know how bad we are. We don't need to be reminded with the law. We already know!

Why are churches preaching law week after week reminding people of their sins instead of pointing them to their savior?! Jesus went to the cross so I would never have to live in guilt, shame, or condemnation! Jesus paid my price. I don't measure up, but in Christ, I totally measure up.

Sigh... that makes me smile!

1 Corinthians 15:56-57...and the power of sin is the law. But thanks be to God! He gives us the victory through our Lord Jesus Christ.

Whoa! Did you see that?! What does the law (The Ten Commandments) give power to? Sin! The law actually gives sin power!

Notice what else it says: Victory comes not from the law, but talking about Jesus! We need to talk less about how bad we are and more about HOW GOOD JESUS IS! This is where your victory is, church. He conquered sin, Satan, and death to give you VICTORY, freedom, and life!

Keep reading; I want to take this even further:

Romans 7:5 ...the sinful passions aroused by the law were at work in our bodies, so that we bore fruit for death.

What does the law do? It arouses us to sin! When you focus on law, you arouse people to sinful passions. The law just makes me want to rebel!

My family was on vacation a while back, and we stayed at a condo in Florida about a block away from the beach. It was beautiful, and the beach was so close! To get there, we just had to walk down a footpath that was between two off-the-hook beachfront mansions. They were amazing! One had an infinity pool out back overlooking the ocean. The other had a magnificent back porch to sit on for watching the waves.

On the little footpath between the two homes, was this sign: NO TRESPASSING.

Guess what did this rule did to me? Well, if you know me, you know that I hate rules! So, I immediately said to Kelly, "Ya dare me to go jump in those people's pool? I bet I could be over this fence, in the pool and back here again before they would ever know!"

She (being the logical one in the family) shut me down fast. "You can't do that! You'll get arrested!"

And I said, "I know. I won't do it."

Pause.

"But if you dare me, I'll totally do it!"

Why did I say that? Because the law arouses sin in us! When we see a rule, what do we want to do? Break it! If the sign says DON'T PEE IN OUR POOL, what do you want to do? PEEEEE! It is human nature. Laws arouse us to sin!

I was always taught that the best way to be a good person was to follow the rules, but this doesn't make us good. It makes us either rebels or self-righteous hall monitors that point out everyone else's infractions! The law arouses us to sin!

Read the verse again.

Romans 7:5 ...the sinful passions aroused by the law were at work in our bodies, so that we bore fruit for death.

Notice the law not only arouses us to sin, but it also leads to death. The more you try to keep the rules, the more dead your soul becomes.

Show me a person who is alive spiritually because of the rules of the Bible and I will show you a liar and hypocrite. The only thing rules do is kill your soul. The law brings DEATH!

I told you this before: by the time I was 15, I wanted nothing to do with this rules-driven Christianity. Then one day, at age 17, someone told me, "Don't you know Christianity isn't about rules? It is about a relationship with Christ." That one sentence changed me forever!

And I went, "Really! If that is the case - that Jesus just likes me the way I am - I will give that version of faith a shot!" Jesus drew me to Himself that night by His grace.

Rules drove me toward spiritual death and rebellion. Grace brought me to life, peace, and a relationship with God.

Romans 5:20 The law was added so that the trespass might increase. But where sin increased, grace increased all the more...

God gave us the law to prove we are not that good. Trespass actually increased because of the Ten Commandments, as they aroused our rebellion. God gave us the rules to prove we couldn't keep them.

He had to find a way to combat our sin. So, what did He do? Look at the verse: *Where sin increased, GRACE INCREASED ALL THE MORE!*

God combats sin not with our righteousness, but with His righteousness. Sin is combated with grace, not law!

Now I know what you are thinking. You are thinking: "If we don't give people rules, they will just sin more!" But that is bad logic. The more rules, the more rebellion. This is why political slogans about "Taking America Back For God" never work! Rules and laws don't change people's hearts. Rather, they foster internal rebellion while attempting external control.

God's idea, which is higher than any of our ideas, is to give you grace, more grace, and more grace. You get grace on tap. The more grace He gives you, the more you will not want to live a life of sin, but you will desire to run to His free gift of righteousness!

Romans 7:6 [In Christ] we have been released from the law so that we serve in the new way of the Spirit, and not in the old way of the written code.

Our emphasis as a Christian cannot be the Ten Commandments, because we were RELEASED from them. Why would you want to preach something you are no longer supposed to strive for? People ask me all the time, "Pastor Eric, why do you have tattoos? I thought the Bible says we are not supposed to have tattoos."

To this, I always smile and say, "Do you eat pork?"

They stop for a second and, most of the time, say, "Sure."

"Really? Why? The Old Testament clearly states that it's wrong to eat pork!"

Suddenly a light goes off in their head! "Oh, so we don't have to follow all that..."

We don't have to follow those rules because we have been released from the law. Jesus fulfilled the law so I don't have to follow it! Jesus had no tats and never ate a pig, so that I could have pulled pork sandwiches, and get as many tats as I want! I am not under the law!

But not just those abstract ones. I am not under any of the law. I am released from all of it! Thou shalt not lie, cheat, steal, kill or commit adultery... we are released! Now, does being released from the law make me want to go out and live like a hellion? Heck, NO! I don't want anything to do with that stuff, because sin brings bondage, addiction, natural consequences, pain, and death.

I was freed from sin at the cross. Why would I want to go back to all that pain, hurt, and guilt? God's grace compels me to righteousness!

See, if grace is the truth, then we are not punished for our sins, we are punished by our sins.

God is never going to take his wrath out on us for sinning, but sinning just messes up our lives. Why would I want to do those things? I want to be free!

Galatians 3:11-14 "The righteous will live by faith." The law is not based on faith; on the contrary, "The man who does these things will live by them." Christ redeemed us from the curse of the law by becoming a curse for us, for it is written: "Cursed is everyone who is hung on a tree." He redeemed us in order that the blessing given to Abraham might come to the Gentiles through Christ Jesus...

Let me break this down for you. The law and faith are opposed because the law is not based on faith, but on self-achievement. Faith just rests! It RESTS in the finished work of Christ, so you don't have to try to earn God's favor. You don't have to try to get God to answer your prayers; God is just going to answer your prayers. Faith rests in the fact that what Jesus did was enough!

On the other hand, the law leads to all kinds of achievement and approval addiction. You are always trying to make God happy. You are always hoping He will be good to you. You are constantly working and never resting. Then, if you are like me, eventually you are either burned out or ticked off because it is never enough. There's always one more thing to do. One more thing to achieve. One more thing I could have done better. And I look around to judge myself against everyone else's performance.

These verses say the law is a curse, so when you try to live by it you curse yourself. When I teach you law instead of grace, I curse you! I don't want to be cursed, and I don't want to bring you a curse! So let's leave the law and move on to grace! Let's walk into the blessing God has for us!

Notice the last part of that passage. *Christ redeemed us to bring us the blessing of Abraham!* We will get into this more later, but know this: the same way God blessed Abraham even though Abraham wasn't perfect, is how He wants to bless you even though you're not perfect either!

When we, as Christians, study the redemptive, finished work of Christ - that is, grace - the blessings FLOW!

CHAPTER 5

JESUS IS AGAINST SOMETHING!

"Anything added to grace destroys it…
When law – even God's own law – is added to grace,
His grace ceases to be grace."
- John MacArthur

Jesus is against something, but it is not what you might think. Hint: It's not gay pride events, Disney, lip rings or cocktails.

Jesus is indeed against a cocktail, but it has nothing to do with Jameson and ginger ale. He's against a far more lethal combination: the mixture of law and grace. He doesn't want His followers living with a little bit of law and a little bit of grace because this destroys BOTH! He is against mixture!

Let me give you some verses on this.

Galatians 5:4 For if you are trying to make yourselves right with God by keeping the law, you have been cut off from Christ! You have fallen away from God's grace. (NLT)

Paul has to take it even a step further. He says if you keep trying to go back to law-based religion you are actually cut off from Christ and His grace. He is saying you can't be about saving grace while growing in law. You have to quit trying to get just the right amounts each of law and grace, and move on to GRACE, straight up. Because of the cross. You add your watered-down efforts to his perfect drink, and he cuts you off. Done.

Romans 11:6 And if by grace, then it is no longer of works; otherwise grace is no longer grace. But if it is of works, it is no longer grace; otherwise work is no longer work. (NKJV)

Paul just made this whole law and grace thing crystal clear! You can't have one with the other. Grace can't have law and law can't have grace! God is against the mixture of law and grace!

When, as a church, we teach you grace one week, and we teach you law the next week, you have life in Christ one week and you are put back in bondage the next. One week you are filled with joy and hope, and the next week you feel like you don't measure up again!

I realized how badly I was jacking up law and grace a while back. People would ask me, "Pastor, I want to bring a friend who doesn't know Christ, but what are you going to preach about next week?"

What they were saying was: "Are you going to preach grace and give my friend hope? Or are you going to preach law and yell at us about how we don't measure up?"

I publicly repented of this kind of teaching. I also promised our church I would never preach law at them again. We will not live in a world of mixture and have life one week and death the next. It's always grace, free grace, straight up, from now on.

My friend, Ted Haggard, calls the mixture of law and grace the "Monkey Anointing". This is where most Christians live. The Monkey Anointing works like this: There were two trees in the Garden of Eden: The tree of life, which brought joy, peace, and, well, life! And the tree of the knowledge of good and evil, which brought knowledge of what is good and what is evil, and hence, our ability to judge and condemn.

When Adam and Eve ate from the tree of the knowledge of good and evil, they immediately knew right from wrong and were condemned because they knew they had done wrong. They experienced no life from this tree - only death.

Jesus came so we could be free from the condemnation of knowing good and evil, and we were given life in Christ. His tree was the tree of life. His grace was our cure from the tree of knowledge of good and evil.

When pastors preach law one week and grace the next, they are like monkeys jumping back and forth between the tree of life and the tree of the knowledge of good and evil. We bless people with life and grace one week, and we curse them with the knowledge of good and evil and condemnation the next.

We do not want the Monkey Anointing! WE WANT LIFE AND FREEDOM IN CHRIST!

This understanding that God is against mixing law and grace helps me understand what Jesus was saying:

Matthew 9:17 "...no one puts new wine into old wineskins. The old skins would burst from the pressure, spilling the wine and ruining the skins. New wine must be stored in new wineskins. That way both the wine and the wineskins are preserved." (NLT)

He is saying you cannot put new grace in old law wineskins. You will destroy both.

Kelly is from Alabama, so she loves sweet tea. Recently there was just an inch or so of tea left in the pitcher, so she made a new batch. But rather than pouring out the last bit of the old tea, she just added the new to it. As a result, in about two days, the new gallon was already tasting old because she had mixed the old and the new. We had to throw it all away. By refusing to "waste" what she had before, she had to waste most of the new batch.

So it is with law and grace. You can't keep a little bit of the old way, thinking it still might be good enough. It's not. Take it out and let God fill you completely with his grace. This way both the integrity of the old law and what Jesus accomplished for grace is preserved.

Martin Luther said it like this in his *Commentary on Galatians*: **"The tyranny of the law is not permanent, but must only last until the time of grace!"**

I think this is what Revelation 3:15-17 is about as well: ***"I know all the things you do, that you are neither hot nor cold. I wish you were one or the other! But since you are like lukewarm water, I will spit you out of my mouth!" (NLT)***

I could never figure out why Jesus was so uptight about lukewarm water. Then it hit me! Jesus is against mixture. Lukewarm is a mixture of hot and cold. He wants to be cold in the law, or hot in grace, but mixture is repulsive and the law just leads to death.

Colossians 4:6 Let your conversation be always full of grace, seasoned with salt...

Our conversations are to be full of grace. Most of our words should be about grace and only seasoned with a little bit of salt. In other words, we can talk about law like it is a seasoning. We just sprinkle a little on to get the point across.

For example:

"So we are all imperfect people, right? Anyone perfect? NO. Cool. So let's talk about how Jesus takes imperfect people and miraculously and completely transforms them."

See - little bit of law! Lots of grace!

The law is salt and it needs to only season our full, tasty meal of grace. Too much salt will repel you. Way too much will kill you. We need the salt of the law long enough to say: "We are imperfect." It makes the flavor of the grace so much better. But a meal of pure salt would be just nasty.

In recovery meetings, they say it like this:

"Let's stop talking about the problem and start talking about the solution!"

A-freaking-MEN! Let's talk about the solution of the cross and the hope and blessing we have because we are the righteousness of God in Christ! Jesus is against mixture.

CHAPTER 6

NO MORE BI-POLAR FAITH

*"Nothing else in the world matters but the kindness of grace.
God's gift to suffering mortals."*
- Jack Kerouac

As I began to dig deep and explore the meaning of God's grace, I came upon two of the most profound verses in all of Scripture: John 1:16-17. I want to unpack these two verses for you with this chapter. First let's look at verse 16.

John 1:16 From the fullness of his grace we have all received one blessing after another...

Where do all our blessings come from according to that verse? The fullness of his grace!

Every blessing you have ever received in life is because of God's grace to you: your health, your job, your house, your car, your spouse, your kids, your bank account, your happiness, your laugh, your friends, your day today, your day tomorrow, the air you breathe, the friends you have, the sunrise and sunset; you get the idea. Every good thing in life, every blessing, comes from God's grace.

It is like there is a big keg of grace up in heaven—positioned right above your head—and the more you lean into Jesus and His love for you, the more you tap that keg and the blessings flow! You did nothing to deserve or earn these blessings. They just pour freely and unceasingly to you forever!

As I write this, our country is in the middle of an election. Our President got into trouble the other day because he said to business owners in a speech: "YOU didn't build that! You had the help of your country and your society." The other party, of course, went nuts and responded: "WE DID TOO BUILD THAT!" And they think that business owners built their own success.

What is sad is that both sides missed it. Our society did not give us our blessings, but we also did not earn our own blessings. Both types of thinking are incorrect!

ALL OUR BLESSINGS FLOW FROM CHRIST! We didn't earn them; we didn't receive them from our community or culture. *We are blessed simply because Jesus was cursed!*

Every single blessing we have is because of Jesus and His grace. From the fullness of His grace, we receive one blessing after another. Everything flows from His grace. You didn't build that! We didn't build that. HE BUILT ALL OUR BLESSINGS!

I would guess you and I would live much more grateful, humble, and generous lives if we truly believed that every blessing came from Jesus—not our own strength, wisdom, culture or society.

I would guess we would not look down on people who are less fortunate and call them lazy if we truly believed that all our blessings are a gift, and none of them were earned.

I would guess we would naturally be people of kindness, meekness, and humility if we truly believed that everything we have is from the keg of God's grace.

I used to think that someday in heaven "no one will boast" about how they got there because we were "saved by grace" (Ephesians 2:8-9). Now I realize that this is small-minded grace. Grace means no one can boast on earth either because all our blessings are "from the fullness of his grace." His keg determines all our blessings. None are earned.

But we are not done with these verses yet. The next verse is just as important.

John 1:17 For the law was given through Moses; grace and truth came through Jesus Christ.

John is now contrasting the lawgiver Moses from the Grace-Giver Jesus Christ. The law came through the law-giver Moses. He went up on the mountain and came down with ten rules for humanity. On the other hand, John says, "Grace and truth came through the grace-giver Jesus Christ." Jesus went up on the mountain and came down not with rules and regulations but with grace and truth.

Notice something with me: **Truth is on the side of grace; it is not opposed to grace.**

Over the years I have heard people say: "We need to balance grace with the truth!" As if grace and the truth are opposites. What I believe they're actually saying is: "We need to balance grace with the law." (As if to say, "grace is a *lie*; let me tell you the *truth* of how much work you have to do to make God happy!")

I reject this thinking. Truth is on the side of grace. Grace and truth are the same thing. GRACE IS THE TRUTH! That is the message of cross! The truth is that I am the righteousness of God in Christ Jesus! The truth is that I am forgiven. The truth is that Jesus took my wrath so that I could have God's favor. The blessings of heaven FREELY flow to me, not because of achievement but because of God's grace.

Grace is the truth, the whole truth, and nothing but the truth! We don't need to balance grace with the truth. Grace is totally imbalanced. It is crazy. It is overwhelming goodness, mercy, and favor to sinners who did nothing to deserve it, earn it, or achieve it!

Let me explain why this matters practically. If we believe we need to balance grace and truth, we end up living in bi-polar Christianity, where one second we are trying to *earn* God's approval and blessings, and the next second we are *thanking* Him for them. Achieving in the law one minute, resting in grace the next. One second we say, "We built this," and we look down on those who were too "lazy" to succeed. The next second with humility we say, "Thank you Jesus for your blessings!"

THAT. IS. CRAZY! This is a terrible way to live. This is a terrible way to treat people. Bi-polar Christianity is not the abundant life; it is a terrible life.

What if we stopped living this way, and starting living as if grace is the truth, the whole truth, and nothing but the truth? What if we actually functioned like every blessing flows simply from His grace? You never earned your degree; you received it by His grace. You never built that business; you were blessed with that business by His grace. You never kicked your addiction; you were given freedom by His grace.

This is consistent Christianity. This is humble Christianity. This is abundant living. This is a keg of blessings freely flowing to you and me all day every day because of Jesus' work on the cross.

CHAPTER 7

OLD TESTAMENT EXAMPLES OF GRACE

"Grace is love that seeks you out when you have nothing to give in return. Grace is love coming at you that has nothing to do with you. Grace is being loved when you are unlovable."
- Paul Zahl

I think many times people hear me talk about the greatness of grace and then ask themselves: "What is the point of the Old Testament then? If all is grace, why does the Old Testament even matter?"

And the answer is this:

The Old Testament is FULL of God's grace too. You just have to look for it. It's been said that The Old Testament is God's grace concealed. The New Testament is God's grace revealed!

Let me give you some examples of Grace in the Old Testament:

The Priest

The priest worked in the tabernacle helping the average Hebrew get His sins removed and forgiven by God. He worked all day, 6 days a week, making blood sacrifices for the forgiveness of sin.

He took a lamb,
put the sins of the people on the lamb,
killed a lamb,
burned the lamb,
and said, "You're forgiven."
He took a lamb,
put the sins of the people on the lamb,
killed the lamb,
burned the lamb,
and said, "You're forgiven."
He took a lamb,
put the sins of the people on the lamb,
killed the lamb,
burned the lamb,
and said, "You're forgiven."
He took a lamb,
put the sins of the people on the lamb,
killed the lamb,
burned the lamb,
and said, "You're forgiven."
He took a lamb,

put the sins of the people on the lamb,
killed the lamb,
burned the lamb,
and said, "You're forgiven."

You get the idea. The priest never quit working. He never sat down. There was always more work to do.

It is interesting to note that in the tabernacle there were no chairs for the priest to sit down. The priest was always busy, never finished, because there were always more sins. More sacrifices were always needed.

And then came Jesus. (What a beautiful phrase.) And then came Jesus, the ULTIMATE priest. On our behalf, He made one sacrifice for all time. He died in our place as the Lamb of God. He took all our sins for all of time onto Himself and shouted, "IT IS FINISHED." And then he died.

The sacrifice for all sin, for all time was made. The work was done. And then Scripture says Jesus SAT DOWN at the right hand of the Father.

Here is how Hebrews writes it:

Hebrews 10:12 But when this priest had offered for all time one sacrifice for sins, HE SAT DOWN at the right hand of God.

Jesus was the perfect priest who made the perfect sacrifice as the perfect lamb. He did all the work to get you to heaven. And then He SAT DOWN to show you that the work was done. You do not have to get up and achieve your access to God or heaven or blessing. IT IS FINISHED!

The Ark of the Covenant

You know what the Ark of the Covenant is, right? It is that thing that the Nazis pulled the cover off of in *Indiana Jones and the Raiders of the Lost Ark* and then their faces all melted off. Remember that? Cool. Now just so you know, that face-melting box did not hold ultimate super-power; it held the Ten Commandments.

The top of that Ark thingy was called "The Mercy Seat". It represented the mercy of God.

Once a year the high priest would go into the Holy of Holies where the Ark was kept. He would sprinkle blood from a sacrificial lamb on it seven times and ask God for the forgiveness of the sins of all the people of Israel.

Here's what I find fascinating about this:
The Ten Commandments (the law) were covered with the mercy of God (the mercy seat) and the blood of the lamb. See, even God covers His own law with His mercy and the blood of a lamb.

God's grace always covers the law! I want you to understand that God is not out to expose your sin or point out your failure. Instead, He is out to show Himself capable of covering what you can't seem to hide. He is into covering law and its failure with His mercy and blood.

Even in the Old Testament, God was not a God of rules, but of GRACE!

The Exodus

The Ten Commandments, which is the story of the Exodus, was another movie you probably at least saw in reruns on late-night TV. You know the story: Charlton Heston saw that Israel was in slavery so he went to Pharaoh and said, "LET MY PEOPLE GO!"

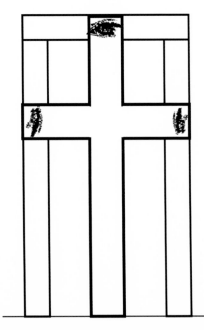

Of course Pharaoh said, "NO!" So, Charlton (Moses) sent ten plagues against Egypt. The final plague was the death of the firstborn sons of Egypt.

But God had a special way of protecting and blessing Israel's firstborn kids so that they did not die in the plague. God told Moses in Exodus 12 that in order to have their kids protected, they must put the blood of a lamb on the doorframe of their home. They were told to put this blood on the top of the doorway, and on the sides of the doorway. The blood from the top would have dripped to the bottom, forming a cross.

Catch this! Israel was protected and blessed because they were under the blood of a lamb.

- They left Egypt protected and blessed under the blood of the lamb!
- Later, when they complained about water, God made bitter waters sweet because they were under the blood. (Exodus 15:25)
- When they complained about having no meat, He gave them meat because they were under the blood. (Exodus 16:11-16)
- When they complained they had no bread, He gave them bread of heaven (manna) because they were under the blood. (Exodus 16:11-16)

But then a sad thing occurred. Moses went up on the mountain and received the two blocks of stone with ten rules on it. The people then arrogantly told God they could follow His rules.

That day God and man made an agreement; they would walk in fellowship by keeping the rules. But they could never follow the rules. They immediately broke them.

- After this, when they complained about their hardships God killed them because they were under the law. (Numbers 11:1-3)
- When they complained about no meat, God killed them because they were under the law. (Numbers 11:33-34)
- When they complained about their leadership, God killed them because they were under the law. (Numbers 16)

Know this: THE LAW KILLS. GRACE BRINGS LIFE.

You can live under the blood of the Lamb and be blessed, or you can live under the curse of the law and be cursed. It is your choice. You can trust His finished work, or you can keep working. Which will you choose?

CHAPTER 8

NEW TESTAMENT EXAMPLES OF GRACE

"Grace is the most perplexing, powerful force in the universe, and, I believe, the only hope for our twisted, violent planet."
- Philip Yancey

Obviously, if Jesus is grace, then the New Testament is full of grace since it is about Jesus. But let me give you some awesome examples.

- The life of Paul. He killed Christians, but then God redeemed him and used him greatly. Grace.
- The life of Peter. He denied Christ three times, but he got another shot. Grace.
- The woman at the well. (John 4) She was totally a home-wrecker, but Jesus loved her and blessed her. Grace.

There are a ton more we could focus on, but I want to continue to contrast law and grace. I think a fantastic example is to compare the rich young ruler and Zacchaeus. Let's talk about these two guys for a minute.

In Luke 18:19-23, a rich young guy comes to Jesus and says, "What must I do to get eternal life?" Jesus replies, "Just keep the law." Or, just follow the Ten Commandments. This dude is stoked, and says, "I have kept them all since I was a kid. I am awesome!" He thinks so because of what he has done. The next four words out of Christ's mouth are devastating and surprising.

Jesus responds by saying, *"ONE THING YOU STILL LACK..."* *-Luke 18:22 (ESV)*

Can you feel the weight of those words? Just one more thing. Oh, you are not quite finished yet. I know you think you have measured up, but there is some more to do! UGH! BACK IN THE DO-DO! I have felt the weight of those words much of my life. I always lack one more thing under the law!

You see, when we try to impress God and keep the law, the only thing we ever hear from God is ONE THING YOU LACK! We never quite arrive. We always have to keep trying.

This leads us to discouragement, which is exactly what happens with the young man in the story. He goes away from Jesus with his head down, sad and disheartened, probably giving up on faith altogether. This is what the law always does. It messes us up. It leaves us discouraged (at best) or angry (at worst) because there is always ONE THING WE LACK.

A while back, Kelly and I had a weekend "off" from church, so we came to the second service on Sunday. Looking to get the full "Crossing" experience, we parked in the main lot and made our way toward the building. As we walked, we noticed a young man we hadn't seen in awhile (we'll call him Joey), just getting in his car to leave after the first service. "How are you?!" we enthused, glad to see him.

"Fine," Joey said dejectedly.

"It's really great to see you at church!"

"Yeah. And now I have yet another challenge that I will totally fail at. Yet again." That day, one of our staff pastors had issued a challenge to do something "big" for God. It was well intentioned, but, just like the guy in scripture, Joey had a faith encounter that left him feeling like "one thing he lacked."

It was that day that we realized even though we are preaching grace alone, it is so easy to slip into "one thing you lack" when challenging believers to walk worthy of the life we've been given. Let us instead be encouraged to give people Zaccheaus stories.

A few verses after Jesus tells the rich young ruler there is one thing he lacks, Christ encounters a dude name Zacchaeus. Zach was a chief tax collector. So, in this culture, he is like a drug kingpin. Everyone hates him. He is a lowlife getting rich off other people. Now this lowlife wants to see Jesus, but he is too short to see over the crowd. So, he climbs a tree to catch a better view. Then Jesus cuts straight through the crowd and stops at his tree and says: *"Zacchaeus, come down immediately. I must stay at your house today." So he came down at once and welcomed him gladly. -Luke 19:5-6*

Notice the word *gladly*! When Jesus gives this guy grace, the response is instantaneous! HE GOT GLAD! That is what grace does! When we receive it from Jesus, even though we all fall short like this guy, we get glad!

Jesus speaks over Zach's life and says: "I don't care what you have done or how far you have fallen. I want to hang out with you. I want to overlook your sin and be your friend!"

I love that. It doesn't even say he pointed out his sin at all! Actually, he ignored it, overlooked it, and didn't care about it at all. He just went right for friendship. That is GRACE! That is what God does for us!

Romans 5:11 He reconciled us to himself through his death on the cross and made us his friends.

Now go back to the story of Zach in Luke 19, notice how the people of the law respond. They get totally upset, bitter, and self-righteous! *All the people saw this and began to mutter, "He has gone to be the guest of a 'sinner'."*

People under law always think they are more spiritual than they really are. They look at the little they happened to get right, look at the other person's sin, and think: "At least I am better than that guy!" They even condemned Jesus Christ! How crazy is that? When you are under law, you can always find fault, even with a perfect person!

But Zach understands he was given grace. Look what he says to Jesus:

Luke 19:8 "Look, Lord! Here and now I give half of my possessions to the poor, and if I have cheated anybody out of anything, I will pay back four times the amount."

ZACH IS A CHANGED MAN! This did not happen because someone pointed out Zach's sin and all the ways he fell short of the law. NO! It happened because Jesus gave him grace and overlooked his sin. And his immediate response is to make his wrongs right, and become a generous man. Law didn't do that. Grace did.

Law leads to a heart that is hard or depressed. Grace leads to change. I know it is true. I have seen the miraculous results of preaching grace as addicts found freedom, lesbians broke up and chose to honor God with their sexuality, murderers confessed (yes, twice I have had people confess murder to me after a grace sermon), and suicidal people gave us the bullets from their guns. All of this happened without mentioning the sins of drug abuse, homosexuality, murder, or suicide.

God's grace can do what the law NEVER can. It can change us from the inside out.

Romans 2:4 It is the goodness of The Lord that leads us to repentance.

I have a friend who was changed dramatically because of grace. I want to share his story with you:

"Basically my whole life I rebelled against authority and I just did not like anybody telling me what to do. You know, I thought I was above that. I thought I was entitled to stuff and that kind of thinking just breeds criminal thoughts. It led me to group up with other criminals and, you know, start doing criminal activity like trafficking drugs. I started out real small, then started pushing my boundaries back slowly. I was stealing small time and small time

using and that led to trafficking weed from Seattle and using Cessna planes to bring that in.

"Things were good. People were making some good money. I was making some good money. I loved the lifestyle. But I was unpredictable and violent. I just... I really confused respect with fear. That's what it was. And I had a lot of people who feared me. And with fear, they would do what I wanted them to do.

"So then eventually I met Jody, who is my wife now. With Jody, I just saw somebody who has stuck by me through everything. She's been through the ringer, man! With a person like that beside you, you want to do right by them, you know? So she talked me into coming to a church that was in a movie theater. That was kind of a weird thing, but I was like, 'Well, whatever. I'll try it, for you.'

"So we started going and the pastor seemed to--Every time I went, Pastor Eric would track me down in the parking lot or in the lobby and that guy--he was just persistent, you know? So yeah, I kept going. I liked to go.

"But even while I was going to church, I still did criminal activity. I was part of robberies and burglaries and selling stolen merchandise and stuff that was a lot smaller than trafficking cocaine.

"So then I got busted again and I went to prison for the second time. I got sentenced to thirty-eight months. After I was in there for about eight months, they offered me a chance to go to boot camp and get an early release. So I went through a six-month program. And things were--I really struggled there. You really had to submit to authority at boot camp, you know? At prison boot camp.

"So, they let me out and a day or two later, I walked into this building and I just couldn't believe it! The little, dinky movie theater church had moved into such a big building. I talked to Pastor Eric, and he was pretty dang excited to see me. You know, I think he was more excited that I was out than I was!

"Things were good. Pastor Eric told me that if I wanted to make this change permanent, I needed to accept Christianity. He knew I was struggling with things and struggling to accept Christ. He said, 'You just have to do it.' So I started out by serving. For about eight or nine months I served as a stage manager. I took the responsibility and tried to do as good of a job as I could.

"And then one day Pastor Kelly called up my wife and told her that she was considering me for a job at The Crossing. And I was like, 'That's unbelievable! This has gotta be a great prank.' But she told me to write up a resume, and I was like, 'Really?' But I wrote up this resume, and it was the most jacked resume possible. I think I listed my special skills as 'evading police' and all my references were prisons like Sing Sing and Folsom. Ha ha! I got buddies that are in Texas in prison, and those are the references I wrote down.

"So I came in and talked to Pastor Eric, and he still hired me! He told me that I had to take a leap of faith. That this is my calling. And so I went home and thought it over. And I told him, 'Yeah, I'm willing to do this.' I faithfully just jumped off the cliff and just let this happen.

"It was at that moment that I truly became a Christian. I was done playing Christian; I'm gonna BE a Christian. Before that it looked like it was an iffy thing. Now I look at it as: this is permanent. The change is permanent for me. I'm a Christian and I'm happy to say that.

"So if you think that you can't change, that you're too embedded in your ways, man you got another thing coming! You just need to try. Just stop playing and accept Christ and accept change. It can stick. You know, life can be great! My life's great, man. I'm jealous of myself! Can't believe what I've got. I've got a beautiful, loving wife. A daughter. I'm just blessed, like every day. Everything that I put out there comes back like ten-fold. Man, I'm just like--I'm just like--man, I'm like the luckiest guy alive, I'll tell you what."

CHAPTER 9

GRACE CHANGED MY VIEW OF THE BIBLE

*"Christ is no Moses, no exactor, no giver of laws,
but a giver of grace, a Savior; he is infinite mercy
and goodness, freely and bountifully given to us."*
- Martin Luther

Once I came to the conclusion that grace is the truth, the whole truth, and nothing but the truth, it changed everything for me. Especially how I read the Bible.

I used to read the Bible and all these verses where God promised to bless the righteous and think: "If only I could be more righteous. If I can just follow all the rules, God will be proud of me!" Now I realize how whacked that kind of thinking is.

I am the righteousness of God (2 Corinthians 5:21), so every verse about God blessing the righteous means He is going to bless me! I don't have to try to get blessed. I just have to BELIEVE the blessings are coming, regardless of my behavior.

We need to read the Bible through the lenses of grace!

Think of it like this: I just got these really cool new Harry Potter-esque round frame glasses. They are a new prescription. When I put them on, the world looks better and more fresh and I'm like, "WHOA!"

That is how we need to read the Bible. We need to read through the lenses of grace. We read not to get blessed, but to know how blessed we already are!

Let me help you. We will practice.

James 5:16 The prayer of a righteous person is powerful and effective.

If you are in Christ, you don't have to try to be more righteous to get your prayer answered. You have Christ's righteousness right now, so all your prayers are powerful and effective!

Believe this truth!

Let's try another one:

Psalm 34:17 The righteous cry out, and the LORD hears them; he delivers them from all their troubles.

Since you are the righteousness of God in Christ Jesus, God hears your prayers and delivers you from all your trouble!

I was taught that God won't hear my prayers if I have sin in my life. That is not true! If you have the righteousness of God, He is listening to your prayers, and He has forgiven all your sin!

Psalm 84:11 The LORD will withhold no good thing from those who do what is right. (NLT)

WHOA! God wants to give me every good thing in life because I am in Christ. Jesus Christ did what is right, so good things are going to flow to me!

Our part is to see the Bible through the lenses of God's GRACE and BELIEVE the GOOD NEWS!

John 6:29 This is the only work God wants from you: Believe in the one he has sent. (NLT)

That's it! Just believe the good news! Good things are coming to you because Jesus did what was right!

This is the gospel! If you are righteous, heaven's doors are opened for you. God's face is turned toward you, your future is bright, you are blessed, and you are going to be blessed even more!

Read the Bible not to see what you should do, but to see what you already have!

CHAPTER 10

GRACE CHANGED MY VIEW OF BLESSINGS

*"Grace is wild. Grace unsettles everything.
Grace overflows the banks. Grace messes up your hair.
Grace is not tame. In fact, unless we are making the
devout nervous, we are not preaching grace as we ought."*
- Doug Wilson

I know I have already gone over this, but I want to be clear. Most people assume obedience brings a blessing, and disobedience brings a punishment from God. I actually found an old sermon from the 90's where I preached that. ICK!

That is law-based thinking and we are not under law! We are under grace.

Jesus obeyed. Therefore, if you are in Christ, you always qualify for a blessing! There is not cursing coming your way. God is never mad at you. He is never disappointed in you. He is never frustrated and wanting you to get off your arse and get to work!

Jesus did the work for you to get blessed. He said, "IT IS FINISHED!"

If that is the case (that the work is done and the obedience has been accomplished), as long as I am in Christ, then the blessings of the law fall on me!

I really want to share this truth with you:

Galatians 3:14 He redeemed us in order that the blessing given to Abraham might come to the Gentiles through Christ Jesus.

Christ died so that the blessing given to Abraham could come to you and me. Well, what did God bless Abraham with? To answer that, you need to read what God says in Genesis 12:2-3.

Genesis 12:2-3 "I will make you into a great nation and I will bless you; I will make your name great, and you will be a blessing. I will bless those who bless you, and whoever curses you I will curse; and all peoples on earth will be blessed through you."

In this passage, God speaks the word "blessing" five times! Five times God promises a blessing to Abraham. The word "*bless*" in Hebrew is the word *barakah*. This word means "*an oath resulting in peace, prosperity, freedom, and safety*"!

This mean that at the cross God promised to you the same promise He gave to Abraham. This promise grants you several supernatural blessings:

Peace. God promised Abraham peace from his enemies, and peace in the middle of tough circumstances. I think this was why Abraham calmly took Isaac up on the mountain. God gave him supernatural peace. He gave you and I the same thing at the cross. The promise of Abraham flows to you! So, what are you so worried about in life? Stop looking at your problems and rest in the finished, perfect work of Christ who gives you peace!

Prosperity. No doubt about it, God blessed old Abe with prosperity. That dude had bank! Now the trippy thing (that most Christians want to deny or ignore) is that God promised you this same blessing! He promised you the blessing of prosperity with the cross!

Now whenever I talk about prosperity, some people want to start shouting, "So you are one of *THOSE prosperity-gospel* preachers!" To be honest, I don't even know what that means. There is no such thing as a prosperity gospel; there is just THE GOSPEL! And THE GOSPEL says if I am in Christ, I am going to prosper. The blessing of Abraham flows to me! Either it is true or not. What do you want, a Gospel of cursing and recession? That is the opposite of blessing. How is that good news? IT'S NOT! THE GOSPEL is good news and this includes BLESSING! Galatians 3:14 says that Abraham's blessings are flowing to you and me! REJOICE! You were given Abraham's prosperity at the cross!

What does it mean to be prosperous? Successful, influential, and thriving - moving to a new level of goodness and happiness. That is awesome! Just like He promised that to Abraham, He promised that to you and me with the cross! Believe it! God wants to bless you with prosperity!

I was talking with someone recently who said, "Churches are just trying to make people feel good. You go there [to church] and all you hear about is how God wants to bless you and prosper you and be good to you. They are just watering down the gospel!" NO, WE AREN'T. Grace is the truth! Jesus wants you to be prosperous and successful!

Do you really think He is looking at you with all His love and thinking: "Wow, I just really want them to fail. I want them to live discouraged, broken down, ruined lives." NO WAY! If a father wanted that for his kids, we would say he is sick! Yet people view God this way. That is sick!

God wants to bless you, which includes prosperity! In Christ, you will be better off, not worse!

Freedom. At the cross, God broke the chains that hold you back. You are free of your addictions at the cross. You are free of your bad habits at the cross. You are free of your hurts and baggage at the cross. You are free of your negative mindsets and bad reputation at the cross. God freed you from bondage at the cross. Why are you working to be free if you are already free?

That is like being a slave who was granted freedom, but then went back to work for his master trying to earn his freedom because it didn't feel right to just accept it. ACCEPT WHAT GOD GAVE YOU! YOU ARE FREE IN JESUS' NAME! This is so important for all my addict friends to catch! If you are free in Christ, why are you relying on the twelve steps? Either you're free or you're not. Which are you? Don't say, "We need Jesus AND we need to work the steps." It is one or the other. You can't believe you have freedom in Christ and then rely on the steps to give you sobriety.

At The Crossing, we rewrote the steps to reflect the grace of God for our Crossing Recovery program. We use the phrase "**Stay in the Flow and You Will Grow.**" If you stay focused on God's grace, it's like floating down a river in a canoe and passing mile markers along the way. These mile markers* will let you know that you are making progress toward freedom.

Safety. God protected Abraham over and over again in his life. From an evil pharaoh who wanted to steal his wife to a guy named Abimelech who kept messing with him to fights with bandits that stole from them. In all this, God was watching out for him. God is doing the same for you. If you are in Christ, the same blessing of safety was spoken over your life.

Ever wonder why Abraham and Sarah lived so long? It was the blessing of God. You were given a blessing of health at the cross. Don't let sickness or disease keep you from all that God has for you. Believe you are healed. Accept His healing, and live! You were promised safety at the cross! Trust that no matter what happens, you will see God's hand of healing in your life.

God promised Abraham peace, prosperity, freedom, and safety. Through Jesus, we are heirs of the promise to Abraham. This means peace, prosperity, freedom, and safety were all promised to you at the cross. Why on earth wouldn't you claim that Good News that God speaks over your life?

This week, walk in faith that the blessings of God are flowing to you because the favor (grace) of God is on you!

*See appendix for a list of the Twelve Mile Markers of Freedom.

CHAPTER 11

[P.S. DON'T SHORTCHANGE YOUR BLESSINGS]

"Grace is a system of living whereby God blesses us because we are in Jesus Christ, and for no other reason at all."
- Steve McVey

I heard a story recently of a family that had booked passage from Europe to America on an ocean liner. They had just enough money for the tickets and some left over to buy some cheese and crackers to eat during their voyage. After three weeks at sea they were weary of cheese and crackers, so they asked the captain what it would cost to eat in the dining hall. The captain was stunned and replied, "What? You don't have to pay to eat in the dining hall. That was included in the price of your ticket!"

This family had been living on cheese and crackers when they had available the entire storehouse of the kitchen!

The same is true for you! You have all the storehouses of heaven available to you. Don't live on the crackers of blessing when you have been promised so much more!

Jesus paid the price so the blessings could flow to you! These blessings are UNEARNED.

What did Abraham do to earn his blessing? Nothing! For all we know, Abraham might have been a pimp or a drug-dealer before God called him. See, Abraham did nothing to deserve the blessing. God just came to him one day and said: "I want to bless you, bless you, bless you, bless you, bless you. What do you think?" And Abe said: "I RECEIVE IT!"

That is all you have to do today to receive peace, prosperity, freedom, and safety, too! You just say, "I BELIEVE IT AND RECEIVE IT!" You rest living in the blessings of your God which you neither earned nor deserve. God did this for you, not because you were good, but because He is good!

These blessings are BIG.

What most Christians say is this: "I believe I am forgiven of my past." For some reason, this is an easy thing to believe. I believe I'm forgiven. So they believe just one small part of a much larger blessing. It's like only seeing one lake when you visit Minnesota. It's like only riding one coaster at Busch Gardens. It's like going to Old Country Buffet and only eating the salad. There is so much more! Believe the entirety of grace!

You were given the blessing of Abraham. Why would you just want to accept the blessing of forgiveness and skip out on the all the other good stuff? Don't believe the lie of the evil one that tells you: "You are forgiven, but you have to wait 'til the next life to really live."

NO! Jesus says in **John 10:10, "I have come that they might have life, and that they may have it ABUNDANTLY!" (NKJV)**

He wants to bless you with more than forgiveness. He wants to give you an abundant life beyond what you could ask or imagine.

These blessings are YES!

2 Corinthians 1:20-21 For no matter how many promises God has made, they are "Yes" in Christ. And so through him the "Amen" is spoken by us to the glory of God.

Notice that if you are "in Christ", all the promises in the Bible are "YES" FOR YOU! All of them. If He spoke them over someone else, they are YES for you! You never have to wonder if God wants to be good to you. Every promise in the Book is YES! Not maybe or possibly, but YES!

However, for it to come to pass you must believe it. The last part of the verse says: **...through him the "Amen" is spoken by us to the glory of God.**

AMEN means "So be it". Or, I believe it. We must SPEAK OUR BELIEF in order for the blessings to flow. This is how we bring glory to God. We don't *do* a bunch of stuff. We don't work really hard. We just hear what He has to say, and reply, "So be it," to whatever it is. You want your life to glorify God? Say yes to His blessings.

I dare you to speak this out loud right now:

I believe that all the promises in the Bible are "Yes" to me. Specifically, I believe Jesus died to forgive my sin and give me His righteousness. I am the righteousness of God!

At the cross, I was given the promise of Abraham. I believe I have the peace that was available to Abraham, so I have nothing to worry about.

I believe I have the prosperity of Abraham, so God is going to help the work of my hands succeed. I don't have to worry about my finances, career, or schooling. He is going to make me succeed!

I believe I have the freedom of Abraham. God is going to free me from anything that holds me back. I am an overcomer. I am free and victorious.

I have always been a softy when it comes to outcasts. I was not super popular in high school since I was the weird, conservative kid who was not allowed to do "normal" things.

Because of this, I naturally have a soft spot for outcasts.

I was at a wedding recently and spent most of the evening chatting with a lesbian couple, learning from them how to make homemade wine. My wife and I were some of the only Christian people at the wedding who would even talk to them.

Judgmentalism really bothers me.

I love that The Crossing Church needs cigarette butt containers outside the entrances. I love that people swear when they are around me and don't treat me like some uber holy super spiritual guy. I love that some of the worst "sinners" in our city call me their friend. I love that I'm one of the worst sinners, and Jesus calls me friend.

I love to give grace to people who need it.

But one day recently, I realized that I give ZERO grace to other Christians.

I think this is because I was taught that Christians should "get" it. They are already in Christ. They already know of God's grace. So if they are being mean or judgmental or lazy or disobedient, it is because they are basically self-righteous jerks who need to get off their butts and love Jesus.

I gave grace to everyone but Christians. Once you accept grace and become a Christian, you get law. No soup for you! (Yes, I am a *Seinfeld* fan.)

To be fair, I thought this way because I saw how Jesus handled the Pharisees. He said things to them like: ***"You are a sons of hell! You are hypocrites!" (Matthew 23)***, so I thought that was how I was supposed to treat religious people. They were jerks coated in religion.

But there are a couple flaws with this thinking:

1. I am not Jesus, and I am a hypocrite, so who am I to call anyone else that?

2. Jesus was yelling at people under law, and we are under grace, not law.

Once I better understood grace, I realized that grace is for EVERYONE, not just non-Christians!

Ugh. Woe is me, for I get it so wrong, so often!

Originally, we come to Christ because of His great grace, but the only way we stay in Christ is by living in gratitude of grace. We can never obey enough to be worthy of "Well done, good and faithful servant." We just receive this word over our life, no matter our actions, because of the cross.

So, I recently made this vow in front of our church:

I repent of giving grace to seekers and law to believers. I WILL NEVER "SHOULD" ON ANYONE AGAIN!

A basic definition for those of you that are unfamiliar with "should-ing": Telling someone, "You SHOULD change! You SHOULD try harder! You SHOULD, you SHOULD, you SHOULD…" Well, you get the idea.

I refuse to be a preacher who "shoulds" all over people. There are already enough "shoulds" in the world. You don't need this at church, too. Grace extends to everyone, not only non-Christians.

And while we are at it: STOP SHOULDING ON YOURSELF! That is just not helpful!

When you read a verse like this:

Matthew 22:37-41 Jesus replied: "Love the Lord your God with all your heart and with all your soul and with all your mind. This is the first and greatest commandment. And the second is like it: Love your neighbor as yourself."

Don't say to yourself: "I *should* love God more and my neighbor more!" Don't should on yourself! You know you are not living up to this law. You don't even like your neighbor, let alone love him!

Instead, read the scriptures in light of His grace!

1 John 4:19 We love Him because He first loved us. (NKJV)

We will only love Him to the extent that we understand His love for us. So instead of focusing on your lack of love, focus on His love for you! Focus on the good things He has done lately in your life. Focus on the cross. Focus on his gifts and blessings. As you do this, you will want to love Him back. Preachers won't have to tell you. You won't have to tell yourself. You will just love Him because you understand and feel His great love for you! And once you grasp His love for you, you'll naturally love others as naturally as you love yourself.

Grace doesn't stop at the point of your salvation. By grace you are saved. But also by grace you live! Jesus came so all our shoulding could stop! What great grace for ourselves and everyone we know.

CHAPTER 13

GRACE CHANGES HOW WE DEAL
WITH PEOPLE WHO SIN AGAINST US

*"If the people do not like the doctrine of grace,
give them all the more of it."*
- C. H. Spurgeon

Matthew 18:15-17 "If your brother or sister sins, go and point out their fault, just between the two of you. If they listen to you, you have won them over. But if they will not listen, take one or two others along, so that 'every matter may be established by the testimony of two or three witnesses.' If they still refuse to listen, tell it to the church; and if they refuse to listen even to the church, treat them as you would a pagan or a tax collector."

Long ago I was taught the concept of church discipline based on Matthew 18:15-17:

- If someone is in sin, go talk to them about it one-on-one. (FYI: That is all of us. We are all in sin.)
- If they are unrepentant, go to them a second time with two or three others to convince them. (So you talk about their issues with others and then mob them together.)
- If they are still unrepentant, tell the entire church what a jackass they are. (Publically humiliate them before everyone.)
- If they are STILL unrepentant, KICK THEM OUT OF THE CHURCH! Treat them like pagans and tax collectors. (Everyone knows we Christians hate on anyone who is not as "spiritual" as we are.)

That is how Matthew was taught to me. I am being sarcastic, but not really. That is the heart of what I was taught. And honestly, it would be correct if we were under law, except we AREN'T. We are under grace! So, let me teach you what I've learned about viewing this passage through the lenses of grace:

Matthew 18:15-17 If your brother sins against you, go and show him his fault...
Notice: they actually sinned against you, not just that you were offended by them. They actually did something sinful, hurtful, and evil to you. Grace just gets over offense. Sin and offense are two different things.

...just between the two of you.
So if someone sins against you, you don't tell ANYONE! That would be gossip. Grace covers their sin like the mercy seat covered the law, and doesn't expose it. So you go one-on-one, privately, considerately, and carefully.

If he listens to you, you have won your brother over. But if he will not listen, take one or two others along, so that 'every matter may be established by the testimony of two or three witnesses.'

You tell one or two other people your issue. Together you humbly go again and try to help this person see how they have sinned against you. The good part about this step is that sometimes the one or two others will be wise enough to show you that maybe you are the one in the wrong.

If he refuses to listen to them, tell it to the church...

Let's get something straight: A church in this culture is a group of people meeting in a house, so approximately ten to twelve people. I don't think Jesus meant for us to tell a mega-church someone's sin issues. I don't think Christ was after us blogging and gossiping about someone else's struggles. That doesn't seem consistent with His heart of grace. What I have come to believe that He meant here is: you are to get a church leader, someone who represents the church. Explain to them the situation and then take the leader or pastor with you to go talk to this person privately and carefully again in hopes they will see their fault.

...and if he refuses to listen even to the church, treat him as you would a pagan or a tax collector.

So now I get to kick him out right? I get to stone him, mock him, pick on him and tear him down? No! How did Jesus treat pagans and tax collectors?

I'm gonna give you a minute to think about that...

How did Jesus treat pagans and tax collectors? You got your answer yet? You smellin' what I'm steppin' in? Yes! I see the light dawning across your face, just like it did mine. Jesus was a FRIEND of SINNERS! He just gave them GRACE!

Whoa! So basically what Jesus was saying is to just forgive him, move on, and keep on loving him! Crazy! If people think they are not in the wrong and are unrepentant, we are to forgive them anyway and just move on with our lives, treating them with grace. At this point, we just leave it up to the Holy Spirit to convict their hearts in His timing. How very freeing!

Now I know that some of you will really not believe my interpretation here, and you will try to fight me on it. I want to encourage you to look at the context of this passage.

Remember context is king. If someone's interpretation is not in conTEXT, it is just a CON.

So let's look at the next thing Peter says to Jesus:

Matthew 18:21-22 Then Peter came to Jesus and asked, "Lord, how many times shall I forgive my brother when he sins against me? Up to seven times?" Jesus answered, "I tell you, not seven times, but seventy-seven times."

Peter understood what Jesus meant when He said to treat them as a pagan or tax collector. He knew Jesus just said to forgive them. So he brought not a new topic of conversation, but a follow-up question, "OK, then, how many times to do I have to forgive?"

Jesus responds, "77 times!"

Under law, on the seventy-eighth time, you kick their butt! But, hello, we are not under law, but grace. What Jesus was saying is: Grace has no limits. Mercy has no end. Forgiveness has no boundary. Because God forgave you, you can just forgive every time, no matter what. There is no place for banishment. This is the flow of grace. And I'm so glad, because surely, were it not for grace, I would be banished as well.

Now I know this forgiveness thing is hard for many of us, so I want you to think of it like this. Jesus gave you the gift of forgiveness. It was a present wrapped up in a nice box. You don't have to find forgiveness in yourself for someone else. You just have to open up the present and accept His forgiveness. Once you accept His forgiveness, now you have it in you, and you can just pass it on to someone else.

You don't have to find forgiveness in yourself. You were given it as a gift at the cross. You have HIS forgiveness. Just pass it on to others like it was given to you!

CHAPTER 14

GRACE CHANGED MY VIEW OF FRUIT

"Grace saved my life; it can revolutionize yours."
- Jay Bakker

Galatians 5:22-23 But the fruit of the Spirit is love, joy, peace, forbearance, kindness, goodness, faithfulness, gentleness and self-control. Against such things there is no law.

I never liked studying the fruit of the Spirit passage in Galatians 5. It always made me feel miserable. I would write all those fruit words on my hand in the morning, and at the end of the day, I'd look at the list and smack my head in true Homer-Simpson style, "DOH." I screwed it up again. I am not loving enough, joy-filled enough, peace-filled enough. I suuuuuuuuuck! I really hated that fruit of the Spirit stuff.

Then one day I moved from a life focused on law to one drenched in grace. Once I realized that I'm not supposed to try to grow those fruits—they're who I already am—it changed everything!

Did you know that? You are not trying to be a person of love and joy. It is who you are if you are a Christian! You already ARE those things. They were a gift to you in Jesus!

I like how Joyce Meyer says it: "God never asks something from us, that He did not give us the power to do!"

Or basically, He doesn't want us to try to live out the fruit of the Spirit. He already gave us the fruit of the Spirit. It is all there. We are all those things and now we just GET TO live them out!

Romans 7:6 [In Christ] we have been released from the law so that we serve in the new way of the Spirit, and not in the old way of the written code.

Notice that we serve in the new way of the Spirit. I leave the law and trying so hard behind and just let the Spirit do the work in me. *We serve IN the Spirit, not FOR the Spirit!*

In Christ, the Spirit does the work in me; I don't do the work. This brings so much freedom! I don't have to change me; Jesus' Spirit changes me as I just focus on Christ.

Let's read those fruity verses again:

Galatians 5:22-23 But the fruit of the Spirit is love, joy, peace, patience, kindness, goodness, faithfulness, gentleness and self-control. <u>Against such things there is no law.</u>

There is no law against the fruit of the Spirit. So there is no need for rules when we teach our kids, our students, and our congregations about...

The love of God toward us,
The joy of God about us,
The peace of God for us,
The patience of God with us,
The kindness of God to us,
The goodness of God on us,
The faithfulness of God over us,
The gentleness of God with us, and
The self-control of God in us.

We wouldn't need to give them any laws. If we truly understood these beautiful truths, we would run away from sin and toward Christ and life according to His design. We would embrace all that He is because of all He has done for us.

Grace leads to the fruit of the Spirit in our lives. Or grace IS the fruit of the Spirit.

What?

Let me put it like this:

Love is grace's motivation
Joy is grace smiling
Peace is grace resting
Patience is grace enduring
Kindness is grace in action
Goodness is grace's character
Faithfulness is grace's habit
Gentleness is grace's true touch
Self-control is grace led by the Spirit

Grace changes how we treat people – both sinners and saints. It changes how we treat those that sin against us, and it changes how we teach our families and churches to do what is right.

We do right because He did more than right by us. He gave us grace!

CHAPTER 15

GRACE CHANGED MY VIEW
OF THE PURPOSE OF CHURCH

*"If the gospel isn't good news for everybody,
then it isn't good news for anybody."*
- Rob Bell

I have a confession to make. Fearing that God would not grow our church, I made MISSION the purpose of church. My fear of failure led me to keep evangelism the primary goal at our church.

I drew this diagram:

I said some stuff that I have heard others pastors say:

- We are not an evangelical church; we are missional church! We have a job to do!
- The church does not have a mission; the mission has a church.
- We need to get this job done. We are responsible to save the world from hell.
- It is our job to make Elk River the hardest place on earth to go to hell from.
- My job description is the evangelization of the world before the return of Jesus Christ.
- We can sit around and sing "Kumbaya" in heaven. Right now, we need to move our butts and get this job done!

So we worked hard. We rarely slept. We preached, invited, bribed, gave, and promoted all because we had to accomplish God's mission.

We let mission drive everything.

I see this happen to young church planters all the time. We want to be successful. We don't want to be ten people five years into this thing. We are so afraid we are going to be trapped in a little church so we push and struggle and strive to the point of exhaustion.

Can I just say – STOP IT!

Mission as the center of the church will ruin your relationships. You will have no time for community because you are too busy.

Mission as the center of your church will ruin your marriage. You will be so busy saving the world that you will neglect the one you love the most. At best, you become little more than partners in the work. At worst, you become enemies because of the work.

Mission as the center of your church will ruin your kids. You will be so focused that you won't enjoy the few precious years you get with your children.

Mission as the center of your church will ruin your health. You will be sick, tired, over-caffeinated, high cholesterol-ed, and sore-throated from preaching, working, straining all the time.

Mission as the center of your church will ruin your joy. You will be stressed and worried, emotionally unstable, often depressed, and frustrated most of the time.

This I know to be true. This was me. If you are always on a mission and trying not to fail, it is exhausting. For one called to be a life-giver, I sure was good at giving up the life I was supposed to have "abundantly" "to the full"...for the sake of the mission.

I used to say, "This is the best job in the world!" But I never enjoyed it because I had to keep it all running all the time! It was always: *"One thing you lack."* One more thing to do. One more person to reach. One more problem to solve. One more call to make. One more. One more. One more.

And then one day as I was studying, I was smacked upside the head with grace. And the practical, day-to-day implication of grace.

I don't have to achieve! The mission was accomplished at the cross. I am not responsible for the evangelization of the world before the return of Jesus Christ – Jesus is!

I. Am. Not. God. He is.

It is my responsibility to live in the flow of grace and let God worry about all that accomplishment crap.

If grace is the truth, the purpose of the church can't be MISSION since the MISSION OF GOD was ACCOMPLISHED at the cross.

Jesus said in *John 19:30, "It is finished!"*

Either it is finished or it is not!

Why was I working so hard to accomplish something Jesus said was already done?

Remember when President Bush landed on the deck of that aircraft carrier with a big sign that read MISSION ACCOMPLISHED even though the Iraq war wasn't really over yet? That sucked.

When we make mission the point of the church, we are waving a big banner that says JESUS ACCOMPLISHED THE MISSION, then we just go back to war. After a while, this just sucks.

I don't want to live like that. I want His mission accomplished to mean something. I want His words, "It is finished" to mean, "IT IS FINISHED!" I don't want to build my faith around my achievement. I don't want to always have to keep striving like a gerbil on wheel. I want my faith to be built around what He does, not on what I do! I want to rest in His finished work!

This is why Jesus said:

Matthew 11:28-30 "Come to me, all of you who are weary and carry heavy burdens, and I will give you rest. Take my yoke upon you. Let me teach you, because I am humble and gentle, and you will find rest for your souls. For my yoke fits perfectly, and the burden I give you is light." (NLT)

His goal wasn't to free you from the yoke of religion and then give you a new yoke that was just as hard. His goal was to give you rest for your souls! Peace for your heart, joy for your step, strength for an abundant life.

He did the work to give you grace!

Churches that make MISSION the center of the church create attenders and leaders who are always exhausted. They are burned out, worn down, beaten down, and depressed because there is always more to do. And if they mention how tired they are, their loyalty and heart for Jesus is questioned. To "burn out for Jesus" is touted as the highest honor. Martyrs abound, and we scorn the victory He won by trying to win it ourselves.

This is not right! Yes, we are to evangelize the world. However, if MISSION is the center of the church, we are primarily doers and achievers rather than receivers of grace.

Check out what Jesus said about Pharisees:

Matthew 23:4-5 For they bind heavy burdens, hard to bear, and lay them on men's shoulders, but they themselves will not move them with one of their fingers. (NKJV)

I don't want this to be who I am as a leader. I don't want this to be what our church represents. I want people to come to church and have their burdens lifted, not added to.

People should come in the door carrying heavy loads and leave lightened and free having, had their burdens removed by the grace of God.

We cannot make the center of the church MISSION, or it will be built around our achievement instead of His achievement!

Now don't misunderstand me. My pastor friends reading this are probably freaking out and thinking, "You are bailing on evangelism!" Not at all! I have an evangelist's heart. I want to reach people who are far from God and see them transformed by Christ. I want our church to grow, and I hope and pray every day for this. Our church still advertises in order to reach more people. We still do crazy stuff to share the gospel.

But the point of church is no longer what we DO! It is about what He has already DONE! The point is Him!

So what is the purpose of the church if is it not MISSION?

If grace is the truth, the purpose of the church must be WORSHIP!

As we realize all that God has done for us our hearts, we want to gather with other Christians and celebrate how good God is! We are celebrators of Christ's accomplishment! We are GRACE-REVELERS!

Do you know what a reveler is?

A reveler is someone who needs to calm down! If we understand grace, nothing will settle us down. We will be the wildest, loudest partiers on planet Earth. We will be the most vocal, happy, excited, joy-filled people in existence! Why? Because we were given all the blessings of heaven through the finished work of Christ on the cross!

The Westminster Confession says:

The chief end of man is to glorify God and enjoy Him forever.

In the past, this never made sense to me. I can enjoy God in heaven. Right now I have to tell others about Him.

Now I get it! When I understand grace, I want to worship my Jesus for all He has done for me! The center of the church must be worship.

After we see Jesus and His grace, we will be led to worship, and worship leads us to mission!

See, the disciples ultimately were not fishers of men because Jesus commanded them to do it. They did so out of a grateful, thankful heart overflowing from Jesus' grace.

They watched grace in action.

They heard grace speak.

They witnessed grace's sacrifice.

They saw grace's resurrection power.

They witnessed grace forgive their failures.

Therefore, they could not help but speak of grace to others.

CHAPTER 16

GRACE CHANGED HOW I VIEW LEGALISM

*"Legalism says God will love us if we change.
The gospel says God will change us because He loves us."
- Tullian Tchividjian*

Legalism. I saw it everywhere in my church as a kid. Our church was so strict you had to sign a membership covenant vowing never to play cards, drink, go to movies, or dance. We had a suggested dress code for church services (sport coat preferred), a no-music-with-drums belief (they were invented by the devil), and a boys' hair and girls' skirt length policy for our Christian school. This was our code to be loved by God and to be able to call yourself a Christian.

We had to do these things for God to be pleased with us.

This caused me to seriously rebel, and I didn't find Christ for real until I was seventeen. At seventeen, someone told me that God was not a God of rules, but of relationship. And I dug that. I could handle a God that liked me as I am with all my issues. So I prayed and agreed to make Jesus my forgiver and leader and I started a relationship with Him.

I promptly grew my hair out (early 90's grunge was big then), started going to movies, and listening to Guns N' Roses. And in my mid-20's, I started drinking good, dark beer (Guinness and Sam Adams), and I got my first tattoo.

I was free! I was no longer a legalist! Or so I thought. But I was so wrong.

Legalism is not just about what you drink or whether you get a tattoo. Legalism is a deep-seated belief that in order for God to be pleased with you, you must act a certain way and do certain things. It is a belief that by obedience God is proud of you! And as I grew older I became just as much of a legalist as the people of my old church.

What I became was a MISSIONAL LEGALIST.

I started hearing the word "missional" around 2004. And I loved it. Our churches need to reach people! I need to reach people! Let's invade our cities with the gospel. Now this was all good, but in my mind it moved from "God wants to reach people" to "I only please God if I reach people and fulfill the Great Commission". (Matthew 28:19-20)

I began to believe deeply that it was my personal responsibility to depopulate hell and reach the world for Christ. If I was going to hear, "Well done, good and faithful servant" from Jesus, it started with, "Eric, you better get off your arse and get to work."

And I looked at other churches and other ministries, and I judged them if they were not missional. I became the legalist. It was just a new set of rules for making God happy.

A missional legalist is still just a legalist. It is still believing that you have to do something in order for God to be pleased with you. This is not right. The gospel is this: Jesus did the work, and now God is pleased with me! When Jesus did the work of the cross and said, "IT IS FINISHED" in John 19, God forever became pleased with me because He was pleased with Jesus! The work is done. If you are in Christ and Christ completed the work, then God is well-pleased with you!

If I never win another person to the Lord, I will still hear from God, "Well done, good and faithful servant." Why? Because Jesus was good. Jesus was faithful. Jesus was a servant. And His righteousness was applied to me! (*2 Corinthians 5:21*) WOW! THAT IS FREEING! I am not responsible to change every life and reach the whole world. God is! It is His job. It is my job to have faith in Christ and rest in His finished work.

Now, having said that (all my missional friends are freaking out): Is The Crossing still a missional church? YES!

But we are not legalistically missional. We don't have to reach the world; we want to reach the world because Jesus is so good to us! I have a deeper, better motivation for sharing my faith and telling people the Good News of Christ than ever before. I now want to share my faith and help people who are far from God, meet a Jesus who does not want something from them; He simply wants them to stop their striving and rest in His finished work! I get the privilege of telling people, "YOU CAN REST IN CHRIST! YOU DON'T HAVE TO TRY SO HARD! GOD IS WELL-PLEASED WITH YOU!"

What a wonderful place to be! I have no pressure to share the gospel. I *get* to share the gospel—I am deeply compelled to share the gospel out of rich gratitude that God is well-pleased with me.

I came across this statement last week, and I believe it to be true:

Legalism = God's love for you depends on you.
Missional Legalism = Cultural transformation depends on you.
The Truth of The Gospel = JESUS DOES THE WORK.

Lose the legalism and rest in Christ's finished work. Believe Jesus did the work. Rest in His finished work. Join Him in His work to reach the world! You will walk in joy, and get the privilege of watching God work as you flow comfortably in His design for your life! You will have ringside seats to Him changing lives as you trust in Him.

THE CHAPTER BETWEEN 16 & 17: THE "BIG BUT" CHAPTER

QUESTIONS & ANSWERS ABOUT WHAT YOU'VE READ SO FAR

"My life is a witness to vulgar grace - a grace that amazes as it offends. A grace that pays the eager beaver who works all day long the same wage as the grinning drunk who shows up at ten 'til five. A grace that hikes up the robe and runs breakneck toward the prodigal reeking of sin and wraps him up and decides to throw a party, no ifs, ands, or buts."
- Brennan Manning

I like big buts, and I cannot lie... Sorry. Couldn't resist.

Some of you reading this book will feel like the grace I am preaching is too extreme. It will feel like "vulgar grace" to you.

Others will have some big "BUTS" after reading certain chapters. You might think, "BUT what about this? BUT what about that?"

Here is what I want you to know:

If you have a BIG BUT, it's OK! Your big but is good! It means you are thinking for yourself. I am glad that you are processing rather than just swallowing this concept whole.

This book was never designed to give you all the answers about grace and life. It is designed to get you to think, process, and question. Faith, progress, and transformation happen as you ask questions.

I think I have more questions than answers also. I like the tension of not knowing it all.

Many of my friends and family asked good, challenging questions after reading this book.

Because you and I probably won't have a chance to get together and discuss this, I thought I'd try to address honestly and openly the top 10 big BUT questions people have asked me after reading this book.

Know that my answers are not perfect.

Know that I might answer these questions differently six months from now.

Know that I think grace is messy. And I don't have all the answers.

Know that the way I am wired is to be *all or nothing*. For me, PERSONALLY, if I go back to the law, I might hurt people. I might run over people and push too hard and make people feel bad. I don't want to be that kind of preacher. I want to empower people with the Good News of the gospel of grace.

So here goes...

Big But Question # 1: But isn't faith without works dead (James 2:26)? Are you saying I can sit on my butt and say, "I believe," but never do anything, and live like a selfish jerk?

No! That is not what I am saying. What I believe is that when a person encounters the supernatural transforming grace of Jesus they will WANT TO get up serve the world. They will supernaturally be different.

I believe a heart that receives the love of God will want to give the love of God.

Jesus said in *John 7:38 "Whoever believes in me... rivers of living water will flow from within them."*

This is a promise. When you understand grace - when you truly believe the grace of God that was given for you - you WILL change. Rivers of living water will begin to flow out of you.

You will want to serve Christ and obey Christ and give to Christ. You will want to "love your wife like Christ loves the church." You will want to read your Bible to get to know Him, and pray and listen to Him, and maybe even fast if the Spirit leads you to do these things.

But your doing of these things is led by the Spirit - not by your guilty "have to" - to prove your love for God or to earn His approval or blessings.

Instead, you just do it naturally because your heart is changed and empowered to do it.

Ezekiel 36:26-27 And I will give you a new heart, and a new spirit I will put within you. And I will remove the heart of stone from your flesh and give you a heart of flesh. And I will put my Spirit within you, and cause you to walk in my statutes and be careful to obey my rules. (ESV)

Jesus gives you a new heart, He gives you His Spirit, and now you WILL walk in His ways and be obedient. It is a promise.

A person who says I am "under grace" but never changes has never truly encountered grace. (P.S. The way this person changes is not by us giving them law—but rather GREATER GRACE!)

Big But # 2: But what about the law? Are you saying it doesn't matter at all?

NO! The law is good. It is like a mirror. It reveals our faults. We need the law to know that we are jacked. God thought it up. David said in *Psalm 19:7 The law of The Lord is perfect...*

So the law is not a bad thing; it is a good thing! But its purpose is not to fix your problems - only grace can do that.

I don't want to spend the majority of my time teaching law. I want to teach the law long enough to remind people we are sinners, and then I want to move on to the Savior.

People already know they are sinners. They already feel bad enough about themselves. They don't need me to make them feel worse.

Big But # 3: But what about sin? Are you saying we can do whatever we want?

No! I still believe in a literal evangelical interpretation of sin. I believe sin is wrong, and it breaks God's heart. I just don't believe we are punished by God *for* our sins. Jesus took our punishment.

So you might say, "Why not just sin?" Because sin has *natural* consequences. If I kill someone, God forgives me, but that person is still dead. If I commit adultery, I might be forgiven, but I still ruined my marriage and messed up some other person's life. In Christ, we are not punished FOR our sins, but we are punished BY our sins.

We still face the natural consequences of a night out drinking. We hurt both others and ourselves.

Paul said in *Romans 6:1-2 What shall we say, then? Shall we go on sinning so that grace may increase? By no means! We are those who have died to sin; how can we live in it any longer?*

Or we don't want to go on sinning just because we are under grace! Under grace we DIED to sin. We don't want to live like that any longer!

It is funny the people that say, "I can just sleep around; I'm under grace. God will forgive me." Technically that is true, but you are failing to see the consequences of your sin. Sin is forgiven, but if you walk outside of God's design and live a life of disobedience, you will face the natural consequences of your actions. Not only that, but you will miss the ability to thrive in His plan for your life. How very sad.

My prayer for our church is that everyone will know that they are holy and righteous, and because they know this, they want NOTHING to do with sin any longer. They are clean. Why would they want to go back to the pigpen?

Big But # 4: But what about confession? Are you saying we don't need to confess our sins to God or others?

NO! I think we need confession as a tool of connection with God and others. When I am saved, Jesus forgives all my sins—past, present and future. I am cleansed. I am sin-free. But I still need to acknowledge my wrong when it is revealed by the Holy Spirit or others.

For example: If I get in a fight with Kelly, I want to tell God I am sorry and ask His forgiveness so He knows I have realized my error, even if I am already forgiven. I also want to ask Kelly for forgiveness so our relationship can be restored and good. But AFTER I have confessed, I want to remind myself that I am the righteousness of God in Christ Jesus. I am forgiven and approved by God because of Jesus, so I don't wallow in condemnation and self-pity.

Guilt after confession and forgiveness is a tool of the enemy to keep us from walking forward in faith. You can't move on with your life and succeed if you are still laying around in self-pity and condemnation.

One time a woman came to me after a service at a church where I was guest preaching. I had just preached on grace and righteousness and she walked up and said, "Do you really believe all this grace stuff?"

I replied, "Absolutely! She started to shake and cry. Between her tears, she mumbled, "I murdered my husband."

I said, "WHAT?!"

"I murdered my husband," she said, and then added, "It was like three months ago."

Now I had a dilemma: condemn her or point her to the Savior. So I asked her, "Did you ask Jesus to forgive you?"

"Yes!!" she said. "Over and over again I have asked for forgiveness."

I said, "Good, then you are forgiven. I want you to repeat after me, 'I am the righteousness of God in Christ Jesus. I am forgiven. I am approved of by God'."

She couldn't say it, and just kept crying so I tried a different tactic: "Do you know who wrote that verse, 2 Corinthians 5:21, about being the righteousness of God?"

"No," she said.

"Paul wrote it, and he was a murderer too! God has Paul the murderer write about himself and call himself the righteousness of God! If Paul can say that about himself, YOU can say it about yourself! It is who you are! His grace is enough for you too."

I tried a second time. "Repeat after me, 'I am the righteousness of God in Christ Jesus. I am forgiven. I am approved of by God'."

And through her tears she began to say quietly, "I am the righteousness of God. I am forgiven. I am approved of by God." I had her say it again and again and again until light and peace and hope was seen in her eyes. I watched that day as her guilt started to melt, and she began to be free! I then turned her over to her pastor to be cared for.

I want you to know that confession is good. We need to confess our sins. But we must follow our confession with a faith declaration that we are righteous and approved of, or the enemy wins, and we will never move on with our lives!

I think of this verse that Solomon writes:

Proverbs 24:16 Though the righteous fall seven times, they rise again...

When you know you are righteous, you can get up and go on with your life. If you do not know you are forgiven, righteous and approved, you will lay there in your guilt and self-pity until you die.

Confession is good. Confession with a declaration of righteousness on the end is better.

Big But # 5: But how do we grow if we don't have to do anything?

I think that is a flawed question. Scripture says, *Looking to Jesus, the founder and perfecter of our faith... Hebrews 12:2 (ESV)*

Notice Jesus founded your faith. He started it in you. Then notice that he is the PERFECTER of your faith. He makes you grow. He does the work. Not you!

You can't make yourself grow. You can't make yourself change. You must walk in faith that Jesus founded your faith and will perfect your faith. You are not the change-bringer. HE IS!

I love John 14:15. In the ESV it says: *...if you love me, you will keep my commandments.*

I used to read this and think, "If I am a Christian I have to PROVE it with obedience."

But that, I believe, is the wrong interpretation.

I think Christ is giving you a PROMISE! *If you love me, you will supernaturally obey my commands.* If you are in Christ, He will empower you to obedience. You don't have to try to obey. You will just obey!

Why? *Because the Spirit of God lives in you.*

God never gives you a task he does not first give you the power to do. God never commands obedience in the flesh. We would fail. So first He gives us the Holy Spirit. And then we are led by the Holy Spirit to grow and change and do what God wants us to do.

I never want to work for God in my flesh.

Romans 7:18 "In the flesh dwells no good thing." (KJV)

I don't want to work for God and obey God in the flesh. Working for God in the flesh is not obedience; it is disobedience. Why? Because I am called to live by the SPIRIT!

For example, Moses tried in his own strength to free Israel from Egypt. It was a good idea - it just was not Spirit-led, so the result was murder and failure. Forty years later when Moses was led by the Spirit to free Israel, GOD did the work! Miracles happened. The power of God fell, and everyone knew that God had done it.

That is what I want in my life and our church. I want to do "the work of God". But I only want to do what is a GOD idea, not just a GOOD idea.

Big But # 6: But what about tithing, serving, reading the Bible, praying, and fasting? Are you throwing out the Christian disciplines? Doesn't 2 Timothy say we need to "train ourselves to be Godly"?

Yes, it does say that, and I do believe in the Christian disciplines! I get up and read my Bible almost every day. I have a daily prayer list of things I am believing God for. Sometimes I fast. I have practiced tithing 10% to my church since I was a teenager.

But here is the difference: I used to do these things in order that God might bless me. I read my Bible so I could be a good Christian. I prayed so I might get answers. I fasted for miracles. I tithed so that God would give me more.

Now I understand I AM ALREADY BLESSED BECAUSE OF JESUS. I read my Bible to hear how blessed I already am. I pray because a loving God likes to hear my voice and wants to answer me. I fast when I feel the leading of the Spirit. I tithe because I KNOW I am already blessed and will always have "more than enough."

I do not do these things for a blessing. That is Karma: You do good things to receive good things. That is not the gospel. The gospel is: I do these things BECAUSE I AM ALREADY blessed. It is a response to grace.

God is not dangling a carrot of blessing in front of me to get me to obey. Jesus just filled me up with blessings, and then out of the overflow of super-abundant blessing, I WANT to obey.

Big But # 7: But aren't we called to "seek the Lord" and "pursue righteousness"? Are you saying we don't need to do those things?

No! I want to seek the Lord. I want to be in His presence and pursue His heart. But I want to do this not because I have to, but because I have come to understand how loved I am.

I John 4:19 We love Him because He first loved us.

When I get how loved I am by Him, I will naturally want to love him back. I will want to pursue Him and His righteousness.

My pursuit of Him is only fueled when I know He is relentlessly pursuing me.

Big But #8: But aren't we commanded to evangelize and preach the gospel to all nations? Are you saying we shouldn't witness to those far from God?

AHHH! Please don't say that! My heart is for people far from God. I have an evangelist's heart! My favorite thing in the world is watching people walk across the line of faith and give their lives to Christ!

BUT (now I have a big but) I don't want to share the gospel in the flesh! It would be futile and failure to share Christ where the Holy Spirit isn't even leading! I want to be led by the Spirit to share the gospel where He is already working in someone's life.

For example: In the book of Acts, Phillip was led by the Spirit to sit by a road, and when led by the Spirit, He shared the gospel with an Ethiopian eunuch. The eunuch got radically saved.

That is what I want to see happen. I want Spirit-led evangelism, not fleshly-led evangelism.

I don't want to sit by the road of my choosing and just preach in the flesh to everyone. I want to be Spirit-led and Spirit-empowered to preach the gospel.

I love to witness. But witnessing does not make me more loved by God. Witnessing in the flesh is a waste of time. I want to share the gospel, knowing I am already loved by God and thankful for His grace. As I rest in His love, He will lead me to share His love with others. And the gospel will be fruitful and multiply!

Big But #9: But doesn't Christ call us to a life of sacrifice? Obviously, not all people in Christ are prosperous and successful. What about them?

I do think God calls us to a life of sacrifice. But I also believe when God leads me to sacrifice, it won't feel like sacrifice. It will be done with joy, and I will thrive in the middle of the sacrifice.

I believe where God guides, He provides. If He asks for a sacrifice, He provides the sacrifice and the sustenance after the sacrifice. I have nothing to fear, like Abraham with Isaac. God PROVIDED! And this is how God always works.

On prosperity, I would say this:

You are right that not every Christian you know is prosperous and successful *from your perspective.*

What I mean is: From your perspective, some Christians are less prosperous than you. But how do you know your perspective is God's perspective? For example, a guy with two goats in Africa is more prosperous than the guy with one, but both are poor compared to you. Your perspective might be that he is poor, but his perspective in faith might be praise - because he believes he is blessed and prosperous in Christ because God gave him two goats!

Prosperity is a matter of the mind, not income. Don't compare yourself with others. Just look at your life: Are you more blessed and successful because of being in Christ? Of course you are. All your blessings are from Him. He is the giver of every good gift. I don't believe God makes everyone "your version" of rich. But I do believe you are better off in the gospel than you would be apart from the gospel.

Big But #10: But what about the people imprisoned for their faith or those that lost their jobs or status because of persecution? Or those that prayed for healing, and it never happened?

These are actually two different questions. Let me talk about persecution first.

I believe that God allows this to happen for seasons in people's lives. I believe the enemy comes against us and causes real pain and heartache. And for a time these people hurt, but I also believe God redeems our suffering and that in end we will be better off.

Isaiah 59:19 says, "When the enemy shall come in like a flood, the Spirit of the Lord shall lift up a standard against him." (KJV)

Or, our enemy the devil will come against us, BUT (God's promised BIG BUT) the Spirit of The Lord will stop the enemy and overwhelm the situation, redeeming it for our benefit.

I have been through small levels of persecution - slander, lies, false accusations, even some physical threats to my life and family. It was painful. It hurt a lot. But God was faithful; He never left me. In fact, in the middle of my pain, physical blessings fell, my soul was renewed, and my present state is better than my previous state. The Spirit of the Lord came in.

I like how Psalm 23:5 says it:

"You prepare a table before me in the presence of my enemies."

That is what God did for me when the evil one came after me. He prepared a table of blessing for me that the evil one could not touch. Now, this is not everyone's experience, but I only have my own experience to draw from. Each person has his/her own encounter with God to make sense of.

Now don't misunderstand me here. I didn't win the lottery, and I don't believe God has a million dollars and new Corvette for every believe. But I do believe that in the gospel, I am better off in every area of my life—physically, mentally, relationally, financially, emotionally, and spiritually. And I believe unwaveringly that the same is true for you.

Because of Jesus, I am restored, blessed, prosperous, and GRATEFUL!

Now about the healing part of your question:

I believe God heals. I believe when I pray, God answers, and healing takes place. So when someone tells me that they prayed and healing didn't happen, that is not my problem. That is God's. I just believe He heals, and He told me I can pray for healing, and He will answer. It is my job to pray in faith. It is God's job to heal.

Sometimes I see miracles. Sometimes, honestly, I don't. The *why* question I can't answer. All I can do is go off what I know to be true in the Word of God.

God loves me.

God heals.

God told us to pray for healing.

Therefore, in faith, I pray for healing and believe He will do it.

Some day I might write a whole book on healing. For now, the short and sweet version is I believe God heals - and when I pray I believe He is going to do it, because of His grace toward me.

Conclusion:
I'm guessing that some of these answers satisfied you and some did not. But that is all I know right now. Like you, I am still seeking. All I really know is that grace leads me to life, and that is where I want to be. I ALWAYS try to lean into grace. Even if it feels like "vulgar grace" to others.

PART 2: WHAT GRACE SAYS ABOUT ME (AND YOU)

CHAPTER 17

I AM DEEPLY LOVED

*"Define yourself radically as one beloved by God.
This is the true self. Every other identity is illusion."*
- Brennan Manning

Growing up I always knew my parents loved me and were proud of me. In spite of our super strict church, my dad would say to me every night before bed, "Eric, I love you. You are my son, and I am proud of you."

But actions speak louder than words, and the words of my father were overshadowed by the actions of our church.

Our church honored people who were obedient, and castigated people who failed. I remember a girl in our youth group got pregnant, so she had to stand up in front of the church and publicly apologize for embarrassing our church and God.

I learned a powerful lesson that day: God loves you just as long as you don't embarrass Him.

Later, as I learned about grace (first from Phillip Yancey's book *What's So Amazing About Grace*), I came to realize that God loved me with my flaws, not just who I should be without my flaws. But I still thought I had to obey to continue in this love.

My thought was that yes, God loves me. But that doesn't mean He isn't going to lay the smack down if I step out of line. I better obey, or I will be disciplined.

Here's the problem with that: If I am the righteousness of God in Christ Jesus, what is God going to discipline me for? He took my sin and gave me His righteousness, so what can He lay the smack down about? Nothing!

If you are in Christ, God is not going to punish you for your sins – now or ever! He just loves you. He took your punishment at the cross.

Ephesians 3:17-19 I pray that you, being rooted and established in love, may have power, together with all the saints, to grasp how wide and long and high and deep is the love of Christ, and to know this love that surpasses knowledge...

Paul's prayer was that you would know you are deeply loved by God.

How deep is the love of God for us?

The answer is simple: **Deep enough to be safe.**

We have a rope swing over the river at our home. When we moved in, the water was about ten feet deep off the bank. It was deep enough to swing out, let go, hit the water, and be safe. This summer, however, we were in a drought. If you went off our rope swing, you would fall about seven feet and hit about three feet of water. It was not safe.

I think this is how people view God's love. God's love is deep and safe when they are well behaved, but it is shallow and scary when they sin or fail.

This is not true! God's love is totally, completely, relentlessly deep! You float on an endless ocean of God's love. No matter what you do or don't do, no matter what you say or don't say, no matter what you think or don't think, no matter what you drink or don't drink. No matter whom you sleep with or don't sleep with, God just loves you! His love is DEEP!

I believe that fear and anxiety in your life - about your bills, your marriage, your career, or kids—are due to a lack of understanding of how deep and safe God's love is! If you knew how deep His love was for you, you would never worry or stress. You would know that God is going to take good care of you because you are deeply loved!

"Well, Pastor Eric, how deep is His love really?"

Let me give you four ways God's love is deeper than all the other loves in your life.

1. God's love for us is more personal than a parent's love.

When we think about the deepest human love, most people immediately think of their parents. If anyone is going to love you completely, it's going to be mom or dad.

As a father, I love my kids more than just about anything. For example, I have a really bad gag reflex when I smell horrible things. I mean, it's so bad that when it comes to certain smells I have to leave the room or I will throw up all over everything. But even though I have a gag reflex that is crazy powerful, I have still cleaned up my kids' puke and changed their diapers. Why? I love my kids more than anything.

If you throw up or need your diapers changed, I am not your man. Why? I don't love you like I love my kids. I love my kids with a special kind of love.

Here's where I am going with this: God loves my kids better and in a deeper way than I will ever love them. It is much more personal. Let me give you some verses to prove it.

Isaiah 49:15-16 Can a mother forget the baby at her breast and have no compassion on the child she has borne? Though she may forget, I will not forget you! See, I have engraved you on the palms of my hands...

God loves you so much He tattooed your name on His palms! I don't even love my own kids enough to do that. (I heard from a friend that palm tattoos are some of the most painful.)

Matthew 10:30-31 ...even the very hairs of your head are all numbered. So don't be afraid...

God is so devoted to you, He counted every hair on your head. I have never done that for my kids. I love them, but I have never paid such close attention I counted the hairs of their head!

Psalm 56:8 You keep track of all my sorrows. You have collected all my tears in your bottle. (NLT)

God's love for you is so personal, He collected all your tears in a bottle. A parent doesn't even know every tear a child has cried, and many times we are just trying to get a child to quit crying. God, on the other hand, cares about every tear, collects every tear, and was with you as you cried every tear.

Psalm 68:19 Blessed be the Lord, who bears our burdens and carries us day by day... (AMP)

When we were young, our parents carried us, but then we got to an age when they no longer wanted to do that anymore. God, on the other hand, always carries us. He never gets sick of our burdens. He always wants to help.

Romans 8:15 ...you received the Spirit of sonship. And by him we cry, "Abba, Father."

The word *abba* is the word *daddy*. But it is even more personal than that. It is actually more like the word "dada"! It's one of the first words a child speaks (much to the dismay of many mamas). It is extremely personal. God says because we are His children, He wants to be dada to us. He wants to be the first word on our lips. He wants to be closer to us than a father holding his infant. He wants to do what our parents could never totally do: infinitely, deeply, personally love us.

2. God's love for us is more unconditional than a spouse's love.

I love my wife Kelly tons. She is my favorite person on earth. But I do not love her as unconditionally as Jesus loves her.

Romans 5:8 God showed his great love for us by sending Christ to die for us while we were still sinners. (NLT)

Husbands and wives say, "til death do us part," but in reality our love for each other is actually conditional. If our spouse is bad to us long enough and loud enough, we will eventually give up and leave. If your wife cheats on you repeatedly, you will eventually leave her. Why? Because our love is conditional. Eventually, there is a breaking point, because our tolerance is finite. Self-preservation kicks in and the love is broken.

God's love, however, is unconditional. Romans 5:8 says God loved us while we were still sinning! He was not loving us any less, even while we were cheating on Him. He was not going to leave us. In fact, our cheating on Him motivated Him to sacrifice Himself for us! WOW! That is DEEP LOVE!

Romans 8:38-39 For I am convinced that neither death nor life, neither angels nor demons, neither the present nor the future, nor any powers, neither height nor depth, nor anything else in all creation, will be able to separate us from the love of God that is in Christ Jesus our Lord.

I love how this verse takes away any possibility of God giving up on us. He loves us UNCONDITIONALLY. YOU CANNOT OUT-SIN THE LOVE OF GOD! Sin is not as powerful as God's love!

My favorite quote about the love of God comes from Brennan Manning:

God loves you as you are and not as you should be! Do you believe this? That God loves you beyond worthiness and unworthiness, beyond fidelity and infidelity, that He loves you in the morning sun and the evening rain, that He loves you without caution, regret, boundary, limit or breaking point? [1]

Own that thought! Own that truth! God's love is not based on you, it is based on Him. His love does not quit. He just loves you. You cannot get away from His love.

3. God's love for us is more sacrificial than a soldier's love.

A soldier sacrifices himself for his friends, family, and country. He loves them so much he is willing to die for them. (Though ultimately it's a soldier's goal to let the other guy die for his country instead!) Here's how God's love is different: Jesus didn't just die for His friends. His love is so all-encompassing, He sacrificed Himself for His enemies, too!

John 3:16 For God so loved the world that he gave his one and only Son, that whoever believes in him shall not perish but have eternal life.

Jesus loves the world, not just a few people in it. Jesus loves the good people and the bad people. Jesus loves the rich and poor, young and old, black, white, brown, gay, straight, sick or healthy. He loves Democrats, Republicans, Muslims, Christians, Buddhists, Hindus, atheists, skeptics, and pagans. Jesus loves them all!

It is we who have trouble loving the world! Jesus has no trouble with this!

1 John 4:10 This is real love. It is not that we loved God, but that he loved us and sent his Son as a sacrifice to take away our sins. (NLT)

Notice, He loved us when we totally did not love Him! That is some deep love. He sacrificed Himself for us when we didn't even care. When we were murdering Him with our sin, He was loving us.

4. God's love for us is more transformational than all other kinds of love.

When I think of transformation, I think about a butterfly. It starts out as a nasty, crawling caterpillar. Then it enters a cocoon for a while. And finally it emerges from the cocoon to stretch out its wings and fly.

I believe this is what God's love does for us. The more we cocoon ourselves in the love of God, the more we are changed and go from crawling to soaring. We go from creeping through life to flying and thriving in life. We go from ugly to beautiful.

God's love transforms us in ways nothing else will.

Ephesians 1:4 Long ago, even before he made the world, God loved us and chose us in Christ to be holy and without fault in his eyes. (NLT)

His love changes us from flawed to faultless! We are now, in Christ, without fault, in the eyes of a holy God. This is not a someday-transformation. This is the case right now.

Romans 8:35-39 Who shall separate us from the love of Christ? Shall trouble or hardship or persecution or famine or nakedness or danger or sword? ...No, in all these things we are more than conquerors through him who loved us.

His love changes us from victims to victors. From a sticky-footed ground-creeper to a majestic soaring creature. Christ's love transforms us from a helpless state to a conqueror!

I John 4:18 Perfect love drives out fear.

When you know you are loved perfectly, completely, and deeply - you will never live in fear again. You will be completely transformed. I used to think that courage conquered fear. Now I understand that love conquers fear. There's no need to muster up the courage to go on. Just understand how loved you are. The more you know you are loved, the more fear is eradicated from your life.

His love changes everything.

I want to end this chapter by talking to you about John. John was the youngest of the twelve disciples, and he wrote the Gospel of John about the life of Jesus. It is interesting to see how John refers to himself in the book of John. He calls himself "the disciple Jesus loved". In fact, the only time he ever refers to himself, he says he is one Jesus loved. Take a look:

John 13:23 ...the disciple whom Jesus loved...
John 19:26 ...and the disciple whom [Jesus] loved...
John 20:2 ...the other disciple, the one Jesus loved...
John 21:7 Then the disciple whom Jesus loved...
John 21:20 ...the disciple whom Jesus loved...

What if you began thinking of yourself like John thought about himself? John actually believed he was Jesus' favorite! Do you think this affected how he lived his life? Do you think this gave him confidence, a lack of fear, and victory in hardship? I would guess it did. Knowing you are loved by Jesus changes everything.

What if you began to call yourself _____ (write your name here), the disciple Jesus loves? You are _____, Jesus' favorite. This is how Jesus sees you.

Now, some of you are thinking: "Everyone can't be Jesus' favorite!" But you are wrong. Christ is infinite, not finite. He can focus all His love on just you, and, at the same time, focus all His love on someone else. His love never gets split up. It never gets distracted or diluted. It never lessens. You can claim the title of God's favorite because God is infinitely loving you! He is laser-focused on loving you.

How different would your life be if you lived each day believing you were deeply (personally, unconditionally, sacrificially, transformationally) loved by God?

The grace of God says you are deeply loved.

[1] *Relentless Tenderness of Jesus,* © 1986, 2004 by Brenning Manning. Used by permission of Fleming H. Revell, a division of Baker Book House Company, Grand Rapids, MI. All rights reserved.

CHAPTER 18

I AM HIGHLY FAVORED

"You cannot have the Lord and be anything other than highly favored."
- Paul Ellis

Psalm 30:5 His anger lasts only a moment, but his FAVOR lasts a lifetime.

If grace is the truth, then I am highly favored! The verse you just read says God's anger did flash for a moment. It flashed at Jesus on the cross. In one moment, God took out all His wrath and cursed Christ. Jesus was beaten, butchered, and killed for your sin and mine. Then that moment was over and God's wrath against sin was appeased. There was no more anger left to give. Jesus took ALL OF GOD'S WRATH on Himself for a moment at the cross so that God's favor could fall on you for a lifetime.

Grace/Truth = Because Jesus was cursed for a moment, you get favor forever!

How long do you get favor? FOREVER! Jesus got cursed for a moment so you could have favor forever. That is the truth of grace!

Well, what does it mean to be highly favored?

That is what I want to answer with this chapter. I want you to understand the favor that the grace of God brings to you at the cross.

Let's start simple.

1. God's favor means He makes you righteous.
Most people believe that if they can be righteous, God will bring them favor. If I am gooder, God will be gooder to me. If I am badder, God will be badder to me. This is not true. God's favor is not based on your behavior; it is based on His. The more you understand that God just wants to give you favor, the MORE righteous you will become. Favor leads to righteousness; righteousness doesn't lead to favor. Check out the story of Noah:

Genesis 6:8-9 Noah found favor in the eyes of the LORD. This is the account of Noah. Noah was a righteous man, blameless among the people of his time, and he walked with God.

Which happened first for Noah: Favor or righteousness?

Favor! God was good to Noah. God gave Noah favor. Then Noah became a righteous man. When we know God wants to be good to us, when we believe this and receive this from God, we naturally become better people.

Noah didn't get favor for being good. Noah got favor, and then Noah became good!

Let me give you a verse about this in the New Testament:

Philippians 2:13 For God is working in you, giving you the desire to obey him and the power to do what pleases him. (NLT)

See, you become a better person not by trying to be a better person, but by believing God will make you a better person. When you believe God is working in you (not you working on you), you will become a better person.

If you believe God is giving you a desire to obey Him, then you will obey Him. If you believe God is giving you the power to do what pleases Him, then you will please Him. God makes us better people; we don't make ourselves better people. The more we believe God is working in us, the more God transforms us, and we become the righteous people we want to be!

God's favor means God surrounds you. Open your eyes and become FAVOR-MINDED!

Psalm 5:12 For surely, O LORD, you bless the righteous; you surround them with your favor as with a shield.

If grace is the truth, your righteousness was a gift from God, and God surrounds the righteous with a shield. God promises to surround you, immerse you, and cover you with His favor. What if you became favor-minded? If you BELIEVE you are surrounded with favor, you will see favor.

Think of it like this:

If you believe you're surrounded by trouble and live trouble-minded, what will you see? Trouble! All the time! Even when good things happen, you will always see problems because you are trouble-minded.

If you believe you are poor and live poverty-minded, what will you see? Poverty! You will think you are broke no matter how much you have. You will perpetually say, "I don't have enough" because you are poverty-minded.

If you believe people don't like you, and you live enemy-minded, what will you see? Enemies. Enemies, enemies everywhere! You will live your whole life like everyone is out to get you and like everyone hates you. When you treat people like they hate you, they'll often oblige.

But what if you lived every day favor-minded? Like you get favor forever? What would you see all the time, everywhere you looked? Favor. God promises He surrounds you with favor! Look around, open up your eyes, and see it.

I love the story in 2 Kings 6. A man of God, Elisha, is attacked and surrounded by an invading army. Here is how the story unfolds:

2 Kings 6:15-17 When the servant of the man of God got up and went out early the next morning, an army with horses and chariots had surrounded the city. "Oh, my lord, what shall we do?" the servant asked.

The servant is freaked out, worried, and stressed because he is trouble-minded. He sees himself sounded by trouble! But notice Elisha's favor-mindedness.

"Don't be afraid," the prophet answered. "Those who are with us are more than those who are with them." And Elisha prayed, "O LORD, open his eyes so he may see." Then the LORD opened the servant's eyes, and he looked and saw the hills full of horses and chariots of fire all around Elisha.

Though it looked like they were surrounded in the natural by an overwhelming number of enemies, the real truth was they were surrounded with favor! Elisha prays: "Open his eyes so he may see!"

I pray the same over you today. OPEN YOUR EYES AND SEE! You are surrounded with FAVOR! It is in front of you, behind you, over you, under you, and beside you. You are the righteousness of God, and His favor is on you! Ask God for eyes to see it! Become favor-minded.

At my house, we talk a lot about the favor of God. We try to point out God's favor in every unexpected blessing we experience. For example, in the last few weeks:

Managers or owners paid part or all of our bill at Red Lobster, Denny's, and a Chinese buffet. Bam! Favor of God!

One time my son and I went to a Minnesota Twins game. As I was waiting in line for tickets someone said, "Here, I have two tickets right behind home plate. Do you want them?" Bam! Favor of God!

This summer we went to an amusement park in Florida. As we were waiting in line, someone walked up to us and said, "Would you like to skip the lines and cut to the front? We have Speed Passes that we are not using." Bam! We cut in line for free and went to the front! That's favor!

God being good to you and giving you a good deal that you don't deserve.

God being good to you and giving you an exceptional parking spot.

God being good to you and giving you a promotion at work.

God being good to you and giving you an extra discount on a clearance item (that one was for my wife).

ALL THIS IS FAVOR! You are going to be blessed. You are going to be successful. You are going to get benefits others will not get because God favors His kids!

I've heard it put like this: FAVOR ISN'T FAIR. God gives you unfair advantage in life because you are His kid! Because grace is the truth, you are surrounded with favor!

God's favor means He will cause your work to be successful.

This is a concept I never understood before. I thought I had to work to be successful. But if I am highly favored, God will work on my behalf to make my work successful.

Psalm 90:17 May the favor of the Lord our God rest upon us; establish the work of our hands for us — yes, establish the work of our hands.

What the writer of this psalm wants is for God to make His work succeed. He prays it twice hoping God will answer him. But if grace is the truth, I don't have to hope for favor from God; I just receive favor because of Jesus. Of course God will establish the works of my hands, and my work will succeed!

The cross of Christ guarantees my success! Jesus was cursed so His favor could fall on me for a lifetime! Christian, your work will not be futile! You just do the best you can, and God will bless it! You will succeed in Jesus' name!

I love the Old Testament story of Joseph. Joseph was falsely accused of attempted rape and sent to prison. Most of us would have become bitter and angry and questioned God: "God, where is the favor? I served you, and this is how you treat me?"

But not Joseph! Read what happens here:

Genesis 39:20-23 And Joseph's master took him and put him in the prison, a place where the state prisoners were confined; so he was there in the prison. But the Lord was with Joseph, and showed him mercy and loving-kindness and gave him favor in the sight of the warden of the prison. And the warden of the prison committed to Joseph's care all the prisoners who were in the prison; and whatsoever was done there, he was in charge of it. (NKJV)

Even in prison, in a bad situation, Joseph got promoted! Why? Favor. God was with him so he prospered in whatever he did and where ever he went! God caused him to succeed in life, despite the temporary circumstances.

We really can't ignore the fact that Joe still went to prison. God will still allow us to go through tough stuff. But in the middle of our hardship, because God favors us, we have to believe that His desire is that in each situation, we will succeed and even prosper.

My kids love to play with a rubber ball in the swimming pool. Throwing and catching it is fun, but what's more fun is holding it way down under the water, and then suddenly releasing it so it shoots up out of the water and into the air. As one of God's kids, you are like a rubber ball. No matter how many times you get pushed down under the water, you always pop back to the top! God's hand of favor causes you to rise! RECEIVE IT!

The last part of this story with Joseph says just that:

Genesis 39:23 The prison warden paid no attention to anything that was in [Joseph's] charge, for the Lord was with him and made whatever he did to prosper.

God will do the same for you, if you will stay in faith believing. If Jesus died for you, if you are God's righteousness, if grace is the truth, then your work will prosper!

You are going to get that promotion. And even if you don't, it is because God has a better one for you. You are going to graduate. And even if you don't, it is because God has a better job for you outside of college. You are going to get that big sale. And even if you don't, it is only because God has a bigger sale for you.

Business owner - your business is going to grow.

Pastor - your church is going to succeed.

Unemployed - you are going to get a great job!

Why? FAVOR! The works of your hands are established by the Lord!

2. God's favor means God will give you favor with other people.

I spent much of my Christian life believing that if I am a God-follower, it means I will suffer much persecution and many people won't like me. I thought if I loved Jesus, others would be put off by me and hate me. I even heard militant Christians brag about how they were "persecuted" and "mocked" at their workplace, wearing it as some sort of badge of honor. (I later realized that it was their obnoxiousness that earned the persecution, not their faith in a loving God.)

It is true that Christians do face persecution. Many across the world are abused and even martyred for their faith. I have faced persecution of different forms - slander, threats, lies, anger against me. But a life of persecution is not the normal, to-be-expected state of the Christian life! It is the exception, not the rule. For the most part, God not only gives you a favor with Himself, but also with other people! God will cause those around you to LIKE YOU!

This is the story of Jesus' life. Yes, Jesus was persecuted and killed. But during the majority of His life, He was well liked by those around Him.

Luke 2:52 And Jesus grew in wisdom and stature, and in favor with God and men.

Notice, Jesus had favor with God and with people around him! God will do this for you as well. As you become grace-focused and favor-minded, you will notice that your influence with others will grow. People will like you, people will promote you, people will care what you say, and people will respect you and seek you out for advice.

God does this for you because you are His child. Look how this worked in Joseph's life:
Genesis 39:21 But the Lord was with Joseph, and showed him mercy and loving-kindness and gave him favor in the sight of the warden of the prison. (NLT)

Joseph didn't have to manipulate the warden. He didn't have to give him half his dinner. He didn't have to do something for him to get the warden to like him. He just ended up in the prison and God made the warden like him!

God will do the same for you! God's favor means you will experience favor with others! Not seeing it? Ask Him to do it for you.

Think of it like this: God has already put your name on the mind of an influential person. That person will call you and...

...you will get the sale.
...you will get the promotion.
...you will grow your business.
...you will get into that college.
...you will...

You fill in the *"...you will..."* and ask. God will give you influence with others. Believe it!

He has done this for me. People ask me all the time, "How do you have such influential pastor friends? How do you know all these big names in Christianity? How did that happen?" The answer is FAVOR!

Out of nowhere, I have had seriously influential pastors and leaders call me and say, "God told me I am supposed to mentor you and help your church succeed." It was not something I sought out. I asked God to bring me wise mentors, and He did it for me! The truth is, many of these relationships came through "prison experiences" in my life. Doors have opened for me that are unexplainable. And it really is, I believe, because of God's favor! So even if it looks dark for you right now, ask God to move the hearts of those who can help you, and to cause them to look favorably on you.

I am God's child, so He goes before me and gives me influence and favor with others.

God's favor means He is committed to blessing you forever.

I started this chapter by saying you get favor forever. I want to end the chapter saying this again.

Psalm 67:1 May his face shine with favor upon us. (NLT)

The writer of this psalm was hoping for God's face to shine with favor on Him. Because we are after the cross and under the blood of Jesus, we are guaranteed that God's face shines with favor on us.

It makes me think of my relationship with my youngest son, Aidan. I tuck my kids in bed and pray with them every night. I am old fashioned like that. Many times after we pray, he will say, "Dad, will you just lay here with me for a minute?" So I will stretch out on his bed, and he will curl up against me with his head on my chest. I'll put my arm around him and we will just lay there in the dark for a few minutes.

Why does Aidan want this so badly? He wants to know his daddy is paying special attention to him. He wants to know that my face is turned toward him and that my life is focused on his little life.

This is what our God promises us because of the cross. Because Jesus died for our sins, God's face is always turned toward us. His arm is always around us. He is always open for us to climb on His lap and put our head on His chest. He always wants to comfort, love, care, and focus Himself on our life.

You never have to worry about doing life alone. You never have to fear that God doesn't care or isn't listening. Hear me, Christian – God's face is turned toward you!

Like a father cares for a child, God cares for you.

I want to end this chapter with a final verse on how highly favored forever you are!

Isaiah 54:9-10 "Just as I swore in the time of Noah that I will never again let a flood cover the earth, so now I swear I will never again be angry and punish you. For the mountains may move and the hills disappear, but even then my faithful love for you will remain. My covenant of blessing will never be broken," says the Lord who has mercy on you. (NLT)

God promised Noah with an unbreakable vow that he would never destroy the world with a worldwide flood again. God made an unbreakable vow with you as well. His vow for you is better than just 'no flood'. Look what He promised you—that He will never be angry with you! No matter what you do, or where you go, or how you might fail, He will never be angry with you!
God's covenant. God's vow. God's OATH. God's unbreakable promise over you is that He will always bless you! He will always give you favor!

Psalm 30:5 His anger last only a moment, but his FAVOR lasts a lifetime! (NLT)

CHAPTER 19

I AM GREATLY BLESSED

*"I'd be in big trouble if Karma was going to finally be my judge.
I'd be in deep s---.
It doesn't excuse my mistakes, but I'm holding out for grace."*
- Bono

Several years ago, Kelly and I were invited to an all-expenses-paid pastor's retreat center. We drove all evening after preaching all of our weekend services to this place where we were to stay for a week. It was late when we arrived, and we hadn't eaten dinner yet.

We drove up the lane and, because it was dark, the house kind of resembled a Scooby Doo mansion. She looked at me. I looked at her. And we both decided to go eat somewhere before checking in. So we drove back out the driveway and went to dinner at a cheap Chinese place.

We were so scared it wasn't going to be good—we actually left! We had very little money, so we ate some crappy dinner. Eventually we had no choice but to go check in, so we went to the retreat center—only to discover it was absolutely, over-the-top AWESOME!

The mansion was a Victorian masterpiece. The room we were given was complete with gorgeous antique furniture and claw-foot bathtub.

The pantry was supplied with food available to us anytime, including a giant jar of peanut M&M's to eat whenever we wanted (my favorite part).

The freezer was stocked with ice cream and chilled bowls so our ice cream wouldn't melt.

To top it all off, the kitchen served delicious gourmet food created by a personal chef named Mike.

ALL FREE OF CHARGE!

Kelly and I were insanely, over-the-top blessed!

But the sad thing is we could have been blessed sooner if we had just believed we were blessed! This same thing is true for a lot of Christians. Christians talk about blessing, and they show up at church, but we drive away again from the life that is waiting for us because we don't really believe God is going to be that good to us. I think many of us believe that God is the God of the shot-glass blessing. He is the God of "I will give you enough to get by" or "I will drip a little bit of blessing in your direction." The truth is that He's the God of free refills! God wants to flood our lives with blessing!

The truth: As Christians, we ride on an infinite ocean of blessing. If we believed this, we would see this!

Ephesians 1:3 All praise to God the Father of our Lord Jesus Christ, who has blessed us with every spiritual blessing in the heavenly realms because we are united with Christ. (NLT)

When are you blessed? NOW! Not someday! God's blessings are for this life right now.

How many blessings did God give you? Every! All of them! God did not give us a shot glass of blessing. In Christ, we float on infinite oceans of blessing! We are blessed with everything an infinite God could think up to bless us with!

What if you believed that? What if you believe that, because of grace, God had an infinite ocean of blessing for you? I bet it would change everything about your life.

You wouldn't live in worry. Infinitely blessed.

You wouldn't live in fear. Infinitely blessed.

You wouldn't live in petty fighting or manipulation or backstabbing. You are infinitely blessed.

When you know you are greatly blessed, it changes everything.

What kind of blessings did you receive? **Spiritual blessings!**

Hold on now, I know what you're thinking. "Oh. Spiritual blessings. I knew it was too good to be true; this idea that God would flood my life with blessings. They're just spiritual blessings. Like holiness. And the fruit of the Spirit. Yee-haw."

Wait! It is important that you get this! Spiritual blessings are not lesser blessings. They are supernatural, greater blessings that affect the natural!

When God gives you supernatural blessings, they are not theoretical blessings. They are ACTUAL blessings that affect everything about your natural life. God's blessings affect everything. Where you live, what you eat, where you work, what you drive, what your health is like, your relationship with your wife, your kids' education. God's supernatural blessings affect everything about our natural life.

And, these spiritual blessings are good blessings. God is not scheming to mess you up!

I pretty much grew up thinking that if I mess up, God is going to mess me up! He is scheming to give me trials and hardships and pain in order to make me a better person. But God is not up in heaven scheming to be mean to me. He is in heaven scheming to be good to me!

God's supernatural blessings that affect everything in the natural are good blessings! That is the good news. Because of the cross and God's grace, God is scheming to be good to you.

"So, Pastor Eric, what are my supernatural GREATER blessings?"

Let's answer that by reading three verses from the book of Galatians.

Galatians 3:9 All who put their faith in Christ share the same blessing Abraham received because of his faith. (NLT)

Your blessing in Christ is the same blessing Abraham received from God!

Galatians 3:14 Through the work of Christ Jesus, God has blessed [us] with the same blessing he promised to Abraham... (NLT)

Through Jesus and the cross, God gave you the same blessing He promises Abe!

Galatians 3:29 And now that you belong to Christ, you are the true children of Abraham. You are his heirs, and now all the promises God gave to him belong to you. (NLT)

All the promises of blessing that God gave to Abraham, He gave to you in Christ!

Paul tells you three times in one chapter that you get the blessing of Abraham! Authors tend to repeat what is important, so apparently this blessing of yours is a pretty big deal!

YOU ARE THE HEIR of Abraham's blessing!

What is an heir?

An heir is the one named in the last will and testament; the one who inherits the family fortune. Whatever Abraham received from God, you should receive from God!

Genesis 12:2-3 talks about this family fortune. Before you read it, I must tell you two things.

1. *This is a seven-fold blessing. Seven is the number of perfection in the Bible, so this is not just any old blessing. This is a perfect blessing! This is the greatest blessing ever spoken over a human life!*

2. *This is YOUR blessing! If you are in Christ, you are an heir of Abraham's perfect blessing. This blessing wasn't just spoken to Abe; it was spoken over you as well. As you read this, believe this. This is your inheritance in Christ!*

Genesis 12:2-3

"I will make you into a great nation...
Your family of faith will grow numerically. You may be the only one in your family that believes right now. But if you stay in faith, God will grow that faith and someone else will come to faith as well. Keep believing. You are not the only one in your family or work place or neighborhood that will believe. If you are a pastor, your church is going to grow. Keep believing. The promise of Abraham is on your life!

...and I will bless you...
The word for "*bless*" here is *barakah* – an oath resulting in peace, prosperity, freedom, and safety. I wrote about this earlier, but basically God promises you a life of peace in a world of anxiety. A life of prosperity in a world that barely gets by. A life of freedom in a world where people are in bondage to sin and addiction. And a life of safety in a world full of evil and pain. Believe this. The promise of Abraham is on your life.

I will make your name great...
Your influence will increase. We always talk about how we can make God's name great. God promises to make your name great if you will stay in faith! Your influence is going to increase! And you can turn around and point to Him, making His name great!

...and you will be a blessing.
God gives these blessings so that you will naturally desire to bless others. Out of the knowledge that we are greatly blessed, we desire to serve others, give generously, and share our faith with people. The truth is that you float on an ocean of infinite blessing. Once you understand that, it becomes easy to give some of your blessing away. Why? Hello! Because you've got an ocean! But as long as you believe you only have a shot glass of blessing, you can't give to others! The more you know you are blessed, the more you will bless others!

I will bless those who bless you...

The people close to you will be naturally better off because of you. God promises to make your blessing spill out on the people around you. When you bump into others, a little bit of your blessing splashes them. For some of you, this means that the only reason your company is still in business is because you are there. Your blessing spills onto your workplace. For some of you, your school is only doing well because you attend there. For some of you, your non-Christian friends are doing well just because you are in their life. Your blessing spills on those around you.

...and whoever curses you I will curse...

God will deal with the people that hate on you, so you don't have to defend yourself or fight against them. Notice He didn't say you would be free of haters. Even Jesus has haters, so don't think you will be able to avoid it. If you breathe air and interact in our world, someone will not like you. BUT, God promises to curse those who hate you. He promises to bring destruction on those that practice slander and tell lies about you, those who gossip behind your back and try to ruin you. God says you don't have to be mean back to them. You don't have to answer your critics or even worry about people that don't like you, because He will take care of them in His own way. That should get you smiling a little. God likes you, so He will deal with those that don't like you. You can just ignore them and enjoy your life! That is a blessing!

...and all peoples on earth will be blessed through you."

The world will be a better place because of you. I want you to say this out loud right now: The world is a better place because I am in it. Say it louder! THE WORLD IS A BETTER PLACE BECAUSE I AM IN IT! Believe it! It is the truth! You are not an accident. You are not a mistake. God thinks the world is better off because He put you in it!

This seven-fold perfect blessing was given to you because of Jesus and His death on the cross. Now I need to say something that I hope you never forget: DON'T EXCLUDE YOURSELF FROM WHAT GOD HAS INCLUDED YOU IN!

Don't ignore God's blessing, or qualify the blessing and say it doesn't really mean that. No, it does mean this! You were given the perfect blessing of Abraham! Don't exclude yourself from what God included you in. The only one that will keep you from experiencing your blessing is you!

Now I know what some of you are thinking. You are thinking: "Why, Pastor Eric? Why would God be this good to me?"

The answer is simple: Because of Jesus. Because Jesus is that good!

Some of you are still protesting: "But you don't understand. I am not good!"

I gotta tell ya, the truth of grace is that blessings are not based on your goodness, but on His goodness! Jesus was cursed on the cross so you could be blessed in your life. This great blessing from God comes to you through the precious, perfect blood of Jesus.

You are greatly blessed.

Psalm 23:5 says, "My cup runs over." (NKJV)

In Christ, your cup is always full and overflowing. If you believe you have a shot glass, God will overflow your shot glass. If you believe you have a bucket of blessing, God will overfill your bucket. If you believe you have a bathtub, He will overflow your bathtub. But if you believe you have an ocean, He will flood you with oceans of blessing!

Believe it. The truth of grace is that YOUR CUP RUNS OVER!

CHAPTER 20

I AM TOTALLY RIGHTEOUS

"Whatever sins I, you and all of us have done, or will do later, are Christ's own sins as truly as if he himself had done them."
- Martin Luther

I have been shouting about this for the entire book, but I wanted to dedicate a chapter to truly understand what this means for us.

Hebrews 5:13 Anyone who lives on milk, being still an infant, is not acquainted with the teaching about righteousness.

This verse is saying most Christians stay in infancy and never grow into adulthood spiritually because they don't understand what scripture teaches about righteousness!

This chapter is an attempt to get you to leave the milk and move on to meat. It is my prayer that as you read this, you grow up and put on big boy faith. You'll leave the baby food faith behind.

I told you before that Righteous = Not guilty, entirely pleasing to God.

That is what God did for you at the cross. He made you NOT GUILTY, ENTIRELY PLEASING TO GOD! Think of it - when God looks at you, He is totally pleased with you! You make God happy. He is smiling at you. He is proud of you. You are a masterpiece to Him!

Now I know that sounds crazy to us, because we know how imperfect we are, so let me explain how this works. I want to tell you about the craziest gift exchange ever!

Over the years I have been to some pretty weird Christmas gag gift exchanges. One time I received a toilet seat. We got my mom a six-pack of Budweiser as a gag gift one year. (She doesn't drink, and she did not think it was funny.) Once I gave a guy a brick from my back yard. That was pretty funny. I wrapped it up all nice and neat. He got all excited because the present was so heavy, and then he unwrapped it to find a stinkin' brick!

I say all this because at the cross, we gave a pretty ridiculous gift to Jesus. Kind of like a brick or a toilet seat.

At the cross, we gave Jesus our garbage bag of mistakes – past, present and future!

You and I have walked through life carrying all our trash. We have hauled with us our mistakes, regrets, sins, whatever you want to call them. We all have them. At the cross, we gave Jesus this junk as a gift and, out of love, He GLADLY took it. He received our trash as a present and took it away from us so we no longer have to carry it, see it, or feel shame about it.

1 Peter 2:24 He personally carried away our sins in his own body on the cross. (NLT)

I love the word personally. He didn't theoretically carry away our sin. He personally carried my sin. He thought about me at the cross. He thought about my garbage, my regrets, my guilt, and my sin. And He said, "Eric, let me free you from that stuff. I will take away all your sin!" WOW!

Scripture says all we have to do to get this kind of forgiveness from Christ is ask for it:

1 John 1:9 If we confess our sins, he is faithful and just and will forgive us our sins and purify us from ALL unrighteousness.

If we just say, "Here is my junk," He forgives us for our junk! Notice, He doesn't just forgive us for our past sin, but ALL our sin—past, present and future! To Jesus on the cross that day, all my sin was in the future. So when He died, He died for everything I have done wrong and ever will do wrong. My sins are all forgiven. So were yours! He has not just forgiven your past, but your present sin and your future sin as well. You are ENTIRELY FORGIVEN! All you trash was put on Christ at the cross! You are not a sinner in His eyes anymore! You are totally forgiven! You're a saint!

That is our part of the gift exchange at the cross. We gave Jesus all our sin. (Isn't that so very nice of us?) But at the cross He also gave us a gift. This part we don't talk about much.

At the cross, Jesus gave us His perfect righteousness.

Think of it like this: Jesus was perfect. He did everything right. He healed people, forgave people, loved people, and sacrificed for people. This earned God's medal of righteousness. Like an Olympic athlete, Jesus won a gold medal in righteousness. Then, at the cross, He gave this medal to you.

He gave you the credit for all His good works. You got credit for His healing, His forgiveness, His love, and His sacrifices. You were given Jesus' medal of righteousness as a gift!

Now I know some of you think I am smoking crack at this point, so let's just go see what Scripture says!

Romans 5:17 For if, by the trespass of the one man, death reigned through that one man, how much more will those who receive God's abundant provision of grace and of the gift of righteousness [entirely pleasing to God] **reign in life through the one man, Jesus Christ.**

Notice He gave you righteousness as a gift! You can't earn it or deserve it. He gave you a medal of righteousness. You are entirely pleasing to God.

Romans 5:19 For just as through the disobedience of the one man the many were made sinners, so also through the obedience of the one man the many will be made righteous *[entirely pleasing to God].*

Through the obedience of Jesus, you were made entirely pleasing to God!

2 Corinthians 5:21 God made him who had no sin to be sin for us, so that in him we might become the righteousness of God *[entirely pleasing to God].*

You became not just any righteousness, but God's righteousness! He gave you His personal righteousness! When God says, "Hey! Where did I put my medal of righteousness? I misplaced it!" He looks at you, sees you wearing it, and says, "Oh, yeah, there is my righteousness! You're my righteousness!"

When God says, "I am righteous," He looks at you as proof!

At the cross we gave Jesus a bag of garbage, and He gave us His righteous acts! We get credit for all He did! That is the craziest gift exchange ever.

If you are not yet a Christian, pray and ask God to forgive you for your sins, and ask Him for His righteousness. It's all yours. I am believing many of you will stop and pray like this:

"Jesus, forgive me for all my sin! I ask You to give me Your perfect righteousness. I want to become a Christian. I make You my forgiver and leader. Amen."

If you prayed that with whatever faith you have, you received His forgiveness and righteousness! You have it! Write down today's date in the front of this book or your Bible, so you never forget this truth that became yours today.

Now, if you have already made that decision and prayed that prayer and are already a Christian, I have a word from God for you: Don't put Christ's perfect gift of righteousness in the closet and go back to your own self-effort!

Most Christians believe God forgave them and gave them righteousness, but then they put the medal in the closet and go back to their own self-effort and try to earn it. This leads to guilt, spiritual burnout, and modern day Pharisee-ism. Don't put God's gift on the shelf and go out and try to be good! You are already gooder than you will ever achieve in a million years of trying! You are, in God's eyes, as good as Jesus.

It was given to you as a gift at the cross! Walk in it. The apostle Paul spoke about this in Galatians 3 and Philippians 3. Read with me:

Galatians 3:1-3 Oh, foolish Galatians! What magician has cast an evil spell on you? For you used to see the meaning of Jesus Christ's death... Let me ask you this one question: Did you receive the Holy Spirit by keeping the law? Of course not, for the Holy Spirit came upon you only after you believed the message you heard about Christ. Have you lost your senses? After starting your Christian lives in the Spirit, why are you now trying to become perfect by your own human effort? (NLT)

Being saved from a life of sin and death was entirely up to God, but then we go live our lives like righteousness is entirely up to us. No! It is not by our human effort; it is His effort that makes us righteous!

Philippians 3:2-3 Watch out for those dogs, those people who do evil, those mutilators who say you must be circumcised to be saved. For we who worship by the Spirit of God are the ones who are truly circumcised. We rely on what Jesus Christ has done for us. We put no confidence in human effort. (NLT)

It is about what Christ has already done, not about what we do! Don't put confidence in your own human strength.

"But Pastor Eric, what is so wrong with a little self-effort? Why does God's righteousness matter so much?"

That is a good question. Let me tell you why our effort is worthless and His gift of righteousness is all we need.

1. When you believe you have God's righteousness, you have power over your sin!

Some people hear all this and think: Well, if I am totally forgiven and totally righteous, I can just go do what I want! That is crazy thinking. Do you really want to go back to your old life of dysfunction? Just because there is no condemnation from God doesn't mean that it's worth going back to that old life! Do you really want to go back to sleeping around, drinking too much, and living with your bitterness and anger? Do you really want to go back to that? Of course not.

God's gift of righteousness does not give you permission to go out and sin; it gives you power over your sin. You have God's righteousness in you. This means you have all of Christ's power to do the right thing. Before you were a Christian, you were incapable of being good. Now, because of Christ's righteousness, you have all the power you need to do right.

Think of it like this:

When I was a kid, I was worried about passing a test in school. So my dad gave me this magic pencil. He said as long as I took the test with that pencil I would do great. I believed him. Was the pencil magic? No! But the pencil gave me confidence to overcome the worries that would cloud my mind, and I did well.

Jesus didn't give you a magic pencil at the cross. He gave you actual power! He gave you His righteousness, and this gives you the power to do right!

You are not the guy you used to be; you have God's righteousness. You are not that girl anymore; you have God's righteousness. You don't have to go back to that sin. You don't have to back to that struggle. You have been empowered by His righteousness to do right!

Romans 6:14 For sin shall not have dominion over you, for you are not under law but under grace. (NKJV)

Before Christ, sin dominated and ruled over you. Now that you are IN Christ, sin cannot rule over you! Believe it. You dominate over sin. It cannot rule you, beat you, or control you! You have dominion because of His righteousness.

2. When you believe you have God's righteousness, you get off the emotional seesaw of guilt and happiness.

Most of my Christian life I have felt happy when I did something good, and bad when I did something bad. Then I was happy again because I did something good, then bad all over again. I was an emotional basket case. I was actually worse than non-Christians. They do something bad and they don't feel bad! They are stable. Me, I was crazy!

I was always second guessing myself and feeling guilty. Then I felt good, like I was on top of the world. This is because I was living based on my own self-effort! I was living life based on the law. And the law, though good, always just condemned me.

2 Corinthians 3:9 If the ministry that condemns men [law] is glorious, how much more glorious is the ministry that brings righteousness [grace]!

Notice the ministry of the law is good. It can be helpful to be condemned a little and shown our error, but over time we need a better way. However, the ministry that brings righteousness is more glorious! Once I knew I was the righteousness of God, I got off the seesaw of guilt and happiness, and I became stable. I was no longer condemned. I was no longer guilty. I became entirely pleasing to God. I can walk in joy all the time! I can walk in confidence all the time. I can walk in hope and happiness no matter what because I am entirely pleasing to God!

Don't you want off that crazy seesaw of self-effort? Aren't you tired of always trying but never achieving? Stop trying! Rest in His achievement! You have the medal of righteousness.

Romans 4:6-8 King David spoke of this, describing the happiness of an undeserving sinner who is declared to be righteous: "Oh, what joy for those whose disobedience is forgiven, whose sins are put out of sight. Yes, what joy for those whose sin is no longer counted against them by the Lord."

Notice when David was DECLARED righteous (he didn't achieve it) he was happy and filled with joy times two! Authors repeat what is important! His gift of righteousness brought what his ACHIEVEMENT could never bring!

Get off the seesaw and onto faith in your savior! On days when you mess up and have a fight with your wife, say things you regret, or make a bad choice: don't beat yourself up. Jesus was already beat up for your sin. Just say this to yourself out loud:

"Jesus loves me. He died for me. He forgave me, even now in this moment. I am the righteousness of God in Christ Jesus."

Then your soul will be open and overwhelmed with God's goodness. Then the Spirit of God will motivate you to apologize to your wife and walk away from your fight guilt- and condemnation-free.

Out of His great gifts to you, you will give great gifts to each other. Out of a guilt-free soul, you will stop swearing so much. Out of a soul free of condemnation, you will not drink so much. You won't get angry so much. You won't worry so much. Guilt won't change you; GRACE WILL!

Now as soon as you read that, some of you think, "Pastor Eric is getting soft on sin! We need to feel bad and beat ourselves up over our sin." Why? God was already hard on sin! He was hard on Jesus for all my sin! He already beat up Jesus for my sin. Don't nullify the cross and beat yourself down when Jesus already took your beat down. You don't have to be hard on yourself. I don't have to be hard on you for your sin! God was already hard on Jesus!

Get off the seesaw of guilt and happiness! You are the righteousness of God!

3. When you believe you have God's righteousness, you know God welcomes you into His presence!

When you try to achieve righteousness, you never really know how God feels about you, whether He wants to see you or not. Whether He wants to hear from you. But when you receive righteousness, you can be confident that He just adores you!

Psalm 17:15 And I—in righteousness I will see your face.

I know that because I have God's medal of righteousness, God's favor is always facing me. He is always listening to my prayers. He is always paying attention. He is always watching over me. He is always there to help. Why? I have His medal.

I always see His face! I am smiling right now. You can be, too. Just stop trying to achieve, and start resting in the gift of His undivided attention any given moment.

4. When you believe you have God's righteousness, you will see the goodness, favor, and blessings of the Lord!

Why are you deeply loved? You are God's righteousness.
Why are you highly favored? You are God's righteousness.
Why are you greatly blessed? You are God's righteousness.
Why will God always be good to you? Because you are entirely pleasing to Him.

Psalm 37:25 I was young and now I am old, yet I have never seen the righteous forsaken or their children begging bread.

Notice it will never happen; the righteous won't be forsaken. Their kids won't be destitute on the streets! God's medal of righteousness guarantees us the blessing!

It is our ticket to all the riches of heaven. It is our pass to the promises of God. You will see ONLY goodness, favor, and blessing from your God because of the ticket of righteousness.

This is the teaching of righteousness you need to hear to make it your Christian life. Now as soon as I say all this some of you are going: "But Eric, what am I supposed to do? I get it. I am God's righteousness, but what am I supposed to *DO*?"

The answer is simple: BELIEVE. Just believe the Good News!

John 6:29 Jesus answered, "The work of God is this: to believe in the one he has sent."

Your work is simply to believe! Just trust that He made you righteous. Just believe the Good News!

During the reformation of the 1500's, the Catholic Church had started to mix law and grace badly. I think it is interesting that Martin Luther and many others came along and began to say, "No! The gospel is SOLA GRATIA – GRACE ALONE! It is not based on our self-effort."

Then a little later, they said: "The gospel is SOLA FIDE – FAITH ALONE! You must simply have faith (believe) in the grace of God to save you and change you."

What is really interesting is what they never said: "SOLA WORKY – WORK ALONE!" Because that is the opposite of the gospel. Depending on our work is self-righteousness.

That is what got Adam and Eve kicked out of the Garden of Eden. Satan came to Eve and said, "If you eat the fruit, you will be like God." So Eve decided to reach up and try to "be like God" on her own. She was reaching for her own self-righteousness instead of relying on what God had done for her. In an instant, Adam and Eve moved from peace to guilt, from rest to work, from happiness to grief, and from life with God to separation and death.

Don't eat from the tree of the knowledge of good and evil. Don't rely on your own self-effort. Don't try to be righteous. Don't try to be like God! Know that in Christ, you are His righteousness. You are entirely pleasing to God. He will make you like Himself. He will overcome your sin. He will change you and bless you and love you! Believe it!

I want to end this chapter with a verse from Philippians 3. I invite you to read it out loud over yourself several times. This is the truth of God's righteousness:

Philippians 3:9 I know longer count on my own righteousness through obeying the law. Rather, I become righteous [entirely pleasing to God] ***through faith in Christ. (NLT)***

Lose the baby faith and move on to big boy faith!

CHAPTER 21

I AM DESTINED TO REIGN

"For grace is given not because we have done good works, but in order that we may be able to do them."
- Saint Augustine of Hippo

One of my favorite Disney movies when I was a kid was *The Sword in the Stone*. When I was young, we didn't have a VCR, so my parents would drop me off at the library on Saturday mornings where they would show Disney movies to kids. So it was in the Des Moines Public Library that I first watched the story of a young nobody peasant boy who did something no one else could do. He pulled a sword from a stone. That one magical act got him crowned king!

I loved that story! I love stories of peasants moved to the palace. I am a sucker for stuff like this. I bet you are, too. Girls love *Cinderella*. Guys love *Rocky*. These are all basically the same plot line: someone with no power and no future defies all odds, wins in life, and lives happily ever after! We love these stories. I believe the reason we love them is because God wired us to reign in life!

Let's go back to the first man and woman in the Garden of Eden. God looked at Adam and Eve and said:

Genesis 1:28 "Be fruitful and multiply; fill the earth and subdue it; have dominion over the fish of the sea, over the birds of the air, and over every living thing that moves on the earth." (NKJV)

Did you see it? God's heart was for us to rule! To have dominion over this earth and everything on it! We were to reign as kings and queens over this world. But then a sad thing happened: our crown was stolen. We traded our royalty for a piece of bad fruit. We exchanged our place of privilege for sinful struggle. We rebelled against God and ate from the tree we were supposed to leave alone. In that moment, we stopped reigning in this life.

From that moment on, death reigned on this earth. Sin reigned on this earth. Pain reigned on this earth. Disease reigned on this earth. The moment mankind fell, we went from ruling to being ruled. This grieved the heart of God. This was never His intent for us; He had higher hopes for His sons and daughters than the bondage of sin and death. So Christ came to earth, lived a perfect life, and freed us from the dominion of sin and death.

That is the story of the gospel. Your crown was stolen in the garden, but your it was restored at the cross!

This is how the Bible says it:

Romans 5:17 For if, by the trespass of the one man, death reigned through that one man...

Because of Adam, death reigned on this earth.

...how much more will those who receive God's abundant provision of grace and of the gift of righteousness reign in life through the one man, Jesus Christ.

Because of JESUS and His gift of grace and righteousness, once again we get to reign in life! Notice we don't just reign someday in the afterlife. We reign in this life! You were restored to royalty at the cross! Why are you living like a peasant when God restored you to the palace?

Revelation 1:5-6 To Him who loved us and washed us from our sins in His own blood, and has made us kings... (NKJV)

When Jesus died for us, His blood washed away our sins AND MOVED US BACK TO A PLACE OF DOMINION! WE RULE AS KINGS IN LIFE!

My favorite way of saying this is:

When the crown of thorns went on Christ's head, the crown of royalty went on yours!

You are royalty. This changes everything! Say to yourself: "I am a righteous royalty. This was granted to me by Christ Jesus at the cross!" This thought changes everything! I need to be careful how I treat you because you are a son or daughter of the King. You are prince or princess of God Most High!

Think about the royal family in England for a second. No matter what their behavior is like, they are still treated like royalty! Why? Royalty is in their blood! It is who they are, regardless of location or situation.

In the same way, I must treat you like royalty no matter what your behavior is like because you are under the blood. At the cross, Christ's royal heritage was passed to you! So I must treat you with honor, grace, dignity, and respect whether you have behaved nicely toward me or not.

You are a king or queen with Christ because of the cross!

Now some of you are thinking: "So what? Pastor Eric, why does this matter so much?" The answer is simple: If you change the way you see yourself, you will change the trajectory of your life.

This is what I have preached over and over again in our church:

Change your mind, change your life.

Where the mind goes, the man follows.

What you think about, you bring about.

Apply this to me back when I was a new Christian. I thought: "Because of Jesus, today I am destined for pain, but someday I am destined to reign."

My thought was, someday, IN HEAVEN, God will restore me and bless me. But in this life, because I am a Christian, I will be persecuted and hated. Now it is true that Christians face persecution. I have faced it many times myself, but persecution is not my destiny! That is a bump in the road on the way to the palace! Besides, how does it help your life to always be thinking: "Bad things are going to happen to me. I am going to be hated, but Jesus loves me."

NO! That doesn't help you. That makes you trouble-minded. Jesus said, *"In this world you will have trouble, but take heart! I have overcome the world." (John 16:33)* Christ's emphasis was not our trouble, but on our Savior's ability to overcome our trouble!

It is flawed, broken thinking to say, "I am destined for pain!" NO! Reject this thought in the name of Jesus! The truth of God's grace is that you are destined to reign! Believe and live confidently in this.

My thinking has totally changed. Now I believe: "Because of Jesus, I am not destined for pain. I am destined to reign!"

How does this help my life? I may go through moments of pain, but I know I am going through it; I will not be stuck in it! I am part of the royal family, so the privileges of royalty will flow to me if I stay in faith! I will overcome. I will live in victory. I will walk in joy. I will not just barely get by. I will thrive because when the crown of thorns went on Christ's head, the crown of royalty went onto mine! Believe! Change your thinking, change your life.

Now, what do I mean by "reign in life"? I think that is a fair question, so let me see if I can define it for you. "Reigning in life" means: Power and authority to be who God created you to be and do what God created you to do. I want to remind you that the power of the resurrected Christ was made available to you at the cross.

Ephesians 1:19-21 I pray that you will begin to understand the incredible greatness of his power FOR us who believe him. This is the same mighty power that raised Christ from the dead... (NLT)

Notice that Christ's power is for you, and it is not weak power. It is the power of the resurrection. You reign in life to be who God created you to be and do what God created you to do because the POWER of Christ is available to you. You have more than enough strength to do what God wants you to do. You have more than enough courage and grit to overcome your struggles. Why? You have Christ's resurrection power!

You also have Christ's authority.

Matthew 16:19 "I will give you the keys of the kingdom of heaven; whatever you bind on earth will be bound in heaven, and whatever you loose on earth will be loosed in heaven." [See also Matthew 18:18-20]

You were given the keys to all of heaven's resources at the cross. Whatever heaven has available is made available to you. If you bind it on earth, you will find heaven binding it for you. If you loose it on earth, it will come to you on earth.

For example: If you loose problems and troubles on earth, what will you have? Problems and troubles. If you believe this is all you will have, it is what you will always have.

Instead, believe Christ overcomes problems, troubles, and trials, and that He gave you the keys of heaven. Then ask for heaven's power to conquer your earthly troubles and trials, and heaven will come to your rescue and help you.

God will not abandon you. Believe it!

Now I didn't say you get whatever you want whenever you want it. I am not talking about selfishly demanding your way with God. I am just saying to believe the promises of God. Speak the promises of God. He gave you the keys of heaven. Heaven's resources are available to you. Believe this regardless of your circumstances. Whatever you do: Don't stop believing! (Now I have Journey stuck in my head. Yours too? You're welcome.)

Let me give you another verse about this:

John 14:12-14 I tell you the truth, anyone who has faith in me will do what I have been doing. He will do even greater things than these, because I am going to the Father. And I will do whatever you ask in my name, so that the Son may bring glory to the Father. You may ask me for anything in my name, and I will do it.

Jesus says you will do greater things than Him, and you will do it, because whatever you ask in His name, He will do.

When someone says, "Stop in the name of the law!" or "Stop in the name of the king!", people stop. Why? The speaker has the backing and authority of the government! You have the backing and authority of a higher government. You have the backing of all of heaven! So when you pray in the name of Jesus, you are invoking the power of heaven to do what you are asking. When you ask for healing in Jesus' name, Jesus heals. When you ask for protection in Jesus' name, Jesus protects. When you ask for wisdom in Jesus' name, Jesus gives you wisdom.

At the cross, Jesus gave you the right to invoke His name. You, as royalty, have Christ's power and authority to do what God calls you to do and be who God created you to be!

Now some of you are wondering what we, as Christians, have power and authority over. I think three things:

1. Because of Jesus and the cross, you have power and authority over Satan.

Luke 10:18-20 He replied, "I saw Satan fall like lightning from heaven. I have given you authority to trample on snakes and scorpions and to overcome all the power of the enemy; nothing will harm you. However, do not rejoice that the spirits submit to you, but rejoice that your names are written in heaven."

Christ gave His followers authority over Satan and demons. Meaning this: Satan, the father of lies, cannot deceive you! You have the ability to recognize truth from lies and not be trapped in the fog of sin. Satan doesn't ruin people's lives with truth. He ruins their lives with lies. He gets them to believe lies, and this causes them to make poor choices.

For example:
A wife believes the lie: "He never picks his clothes off the floor. He doesn't really love me." So she feels angry and hurt.

A child believes the lie: "My parents are keeping me from all the fun." Then he sneaks out to a party where he gets hammered and does something he later regrets.

An employee believes the lie: "The boss hates me. He is really a jerk!" Then every chance she gets, she fights her boss' leadership and eventually gets fired or passed over for a promotion.

See, Satan doesn't win by telling you to do bad things. He wins when you believe lies. When you believe lies, you make choices to do bad things all on your own! Here is the good news: Because of Jesus, you have the power to recognize the lies that are put in your head, see them for what they are, and reject them in Jesus' name!

Kelly helps me with this all the time. When I start to get discouraged and believe I will never succeed, that I will never accomplish anything, or that my ministry is really just futile, and no one is being helped, she helps me to see that is a lie from the enemy. So I pray in the name of Jesus and reject the lies that I am not valuable, that I am not helping people, and I believe the truth that God is using me, that I am valuable, and that I will succeed.

And as I reject the lies and pray against them, I overcome Satan and walk in victory. You can do the same thing! You have been given authority over the father of lies.

SPEAK THE TRUTH AND SHAME THE DEVIL!

2. Because of Jesus and His grace, you have power and authority over sin.

Romans 6:14 ...sin shall not have dominion over you for you are not under law but under grace.

Grace doesn't give you permission to sin, it gives you power over your sin. Sin does not have dominion over a child of God. You can beat sin. You can beat the thing that holds you back. Not because you are strong, but because you are IN CHRIST, and He gave you His resurrection power and the authority to conquer sin and move past who you used to be.

You are not that guy anymore. You are not that girl anymore. You don't have to go back to that old way of life because of Jesus and His power and authority over you. His power and authority is greater than sin's power and authority.

3. Because of Jesus, you have power and authority over situations or struggles.

Circumstances like sickness, lack, hardship, persecution, and pain do not have power and authority over you. YOU have power and authority over these things.

1 John 5:4-5 ...for everyone born of God overcomes the world...

What are you in Christ? AN OVERCOMER! You may have trouble, pain, lack, sickness, or a whole host of issues against you, but in Christ you are an overcomer! YOU WILL BE VICTORIOUS! How do I know this is true? Read the rest of the verse:

...this is the victory that has overcome the world, even our faith.

Your ability to overcome your struggles is directly tied to your faith! If you believe that Christ has come to bring you victory, and you trust His power, you will overcome. But if you believe you will never get past your situation or struggle, unfortunately, you'll be absolutely right.

Your crown of royalty means that power and authority were given to you to conquer your addiction, rule over your sin struggle, defeat your financial problems, win over your sickness, and move past your persecution to something better. Believe this!

Read this with me:

Isaiah 54:17 But no weapon that is formed against you shall prosper... (AMP)

It doesn't say problems and weapons won't form; it just says they won't succeed. You will face struggles, but those problems will not prosper over you. You are going to prosper over them because you are a royal son or daughter of the King.

...and every tongue that shall rise against you in judgment you shall show to be in the wrong. This [peace, righteousness, security, triumph over opposition] is the heritage of the servants of the Lord...

I like the word "heritage" a lot. It means we have an inheritance. We have been passed down a gift from the Lord. Our gift is that NO WEAPON FORMED AGAINST US WILL PROSPER! You can't lose, long-term. It might look bad now, but the One who conquered the grave is in your corner, and He gave you His authority and power! SO RISE UP! BE STRONG! LIVE LIKE

ROYALTY! DON'T GIVE UP! DON'T GET DISCOURAGED! YOU ARE GOING TO WIN!

Deuteronomy 28:13-14 The LORD will make you the head, not the tail. If you pay attention to the commands of the LORD your God that I give you this day and carefully follow them, you will always be at the top, never at the bottom.

Remember, in Christ you are like a rubber ball in a swimming pool. No matter how many times you're underwater, you will always pop back to the top. That's God's promise to you. No matter how many times a situation or a person pulls you down, you will always rise back to the top. You will never stay at the bottom because you are in Christ and possess Christ's righteousness. You can't lose!

I want to end this chapter getting you to think and reign like David did. David was a nothing backwoods shepherd boy who was anointed king by the prophet, Samuel. (I know, it sounds a whole lot like *The Sword in the Stone*, but this story is legit.)

With Samuel's act of pouring oil on his head, everything for David changed. He went from living as a peasant to living in the palace. All it took was one touch from God, and everything changed for him.

At the cross you got the one touch you needed from your Savior to move from living as a peasant to living at the palace. JESUS RESTORED YOU AT THE CROSS. He removed your shame, gave you His righteousness, and gave you the ability to walk confidently as a son or daughter of the King. Don't live life as a peasant when Jesus gave you the palace! What if you lived and thought like David today? What if you reigned like David?

I want you to read Psalm 23 today and let its words restore you. I believe Psalm 23 is a chapter of confidence, how David reigned in life. I pray that, as you read this chapter, you will choose to reign as he did.

REIGN LIKE DAVID - *PSALM 23 (AMP)*

THE LORD is my Shepherd...

God feeds us, guides us, and shields us. We have nothing to fear.

I shall not lack.

In Christ, we lack no good thing! God will meet all your needs. He will take good care of you. Don't live lacking when GOD says you WILL NOT LACK. Believe it!

He makes me lie down in [fresh, tender] green pastures...

Our lives are fresh; our future is not brown, dead, and stale.

He leads me beside the still and restful waters.

God gives us supernatural, abundant peace. We don't have to live overworked, burnt out, tired lives. That is not from God. God is the God of rest. Stop trying so hard! God will take care of you and your situations, so you can live peacefully.

He refreshes and restores my life...

When we are down or discouraged, we can come to God, and He will refresh and restore us. Apart from Him there is not restoration. In Him our self is restored, renewed, and satisfied!

He leads me in the paths of righteousness [uprightness and right standing with Him - not for my earning it, but] for His name's sake.

Jesus gave us His righteousness as a gift. We didn't earn it. We have received all the benefits of His righteousness.

Yes, though I walk through the [deep, sunless] valley of the shadow of death, I will fear or dread no evil, for You are with me; Your rod [to protect] and Your staff [to guide], they comfort me.

When we face problems, pain, and hardship, Jesus never leaves us. He always protects us and guides us through. Notice, we go through the valley of death, but with Jesus, you never stay there! You will come through your problem, stronger on the other side! He will not leave us in the valley of death!

You prepare a table before me in the presence of my enemies.

I believe many times our greatest blessings happen during our greatest opposition. Our pain becomes our promotion. In my life, some of the greatest gifts God ever gave me have happened during terrible moments of struggle, problems, and pain. I have been over-the-top, abundantly blessed during periods when it felt like everything was against me. Take heart! God will bless you during your pain. Believe it. In Christ, you cannot lose.

You anoint my head with oil...

I am royalty. I am a son of the King. I am adopted into the family of the King of Kings. As royalty, I have nothing to fear, nothing to worry about, my needs are met, and my future is secure. I walk in honor, respect, and dignity. So do you!

...my [brimming] cup runs over.

No matter what size faith we bring to God, He always fills it to overflowing. He abundantly, over-the-top floods our lives, world, family, and church with blessing.

Surely or only goodness, mercy, and unfailing love shall follow me all the days of my life...

God does not chase us down and beat us down. He is not mad at us! He chases us down with goodness, mercy, and unending love. He is scheming only to be good to us.

...and through the length of my days the house of the Lord shall be my dwelling place.

As we stay in the house of God, in the presence of God, in the Word of God, and at the feet of Christ, we WILL see all these blessings be ours. What a good God we get to serve!

Thank you, Jesus, for blessing us so much! Thank you for anointing our lives like you anointed David's. Help us reign like David today, in faith, believing you have good plans for us. We thank you that we are destined to reign!

CHAPTER 22

ALWAYS, ONLY, ABOUT JESUS

"Grace is everywhere, like lenses that go unnoticed because you are looking through them."
- Philip Yancey

When you think about your life, the many benefits you have, and the gifts you have received, I hope you realize these gifts are not based on you and your behavior. God's good gifts are because God is good, not because we are good. So many people have the misguided opinion that they somehow contributed to their own success, and this is just not true. Your success, your blessings - every good gift - is always, only because of Jesus.

I want to tear apart a verse for you that says this better than I ever could.

Romans 11:36 EVERYTHING comes from [Jesus]; EVERYTHING exists by [Jesus'] power and [EVERYTHING] is intended for [Jesus'] glory. (NLT)

This verse has three powerful statements. Let me break them down for you.

Romans 11:36 Everything comes from [Jesus]... (NLT)

How much is everything? EVERYTHING! So ALL good gifts in life are because of Jesus, not because of you! Think about your 'everything' for a second:

If you are married: Ladies, your good marriage is not because you are beautiful and sexy. Men, it is not because you said the right things to win your wife's heart. No, your good marriage is simply a gift from God. Lots of beautiful women have been cheated on and lots of devoted men who were way better than you at loving their wives have had their hearts broken. Your good marriage is simply a gift from Jesus.

If you have kids: Your kids are not good because you are a good parent. Lots of better parents than you have been called to the hospital as their kids OD'd. Your good kids are just a gift from Jesus.

If you have a job and an income: Your income is not because you went to college and got a good job. Your income is not because you were smart enough to find a job or climb the corporate ladder. Your income, career, and paycheck are simply because God blessed you. You could have been born in a country where women are not allowed to go to school and get an education. You could have gotten sick and became unable to hold down a good job. You could have been born with a mental handicap and been unable to learn and go to school. Your job is simply a gift from Jesus.

If you have a house or car: You don't own your car or home because you worked for it. You have a house and a vehicle because God blessed you with it. You could have been born in the slums of Mexico City and lived your life in a cardboard shack. Your home and your car are blessings from the goodness of the Lord, not based on you and your merit.

If you have a special talent: That talent is not because you practiced and were dedicated. God gifted you with that special talent, and as you practiced and dedicated yourself to it, you discovered the gift you already had! That talent is a gift from Christ.

If you have decent health: Your health is not because you exercise and eat right. Many people exercise and eat right and still die from cancer! If you are healthy, it is simply a gift from your Creator! Even your ability to draw a breath is from Him.

Are you getting this? Everything good in your life is a gift from God! If this is true, maybe you could worship Jesus and say thank you! Worship flows from a grateful heart. Gratitude is a result of understanding everything is by His grace!

Now as soon as you read that, some of you are thinking: "I don't have a good job. My wife left me. I didn't graduate from college. I don't have good health. My home was foreclosed on!"

Here is what I want to say to you. This comes from a pastor's heart that loves you: "Stop looking at what you DON'T have and thank Him for what you DO have!"

How does it help to think of your life like a country song? (I have no house, no truck, no wife and no life!) How does it help to look at what you don't have? It doesn't! Where the mind goes, the man follows! So if you think about the negative, you will never be grateful. You will never be able to truly worship and say thank you because you are looking at the down side of life.

Look at the positives! Look at what you do have!

You may not be married, but maybe you have your health!
You may not be healthy, but maybe you have a great family around you.
You many not _____ but you do have _____!

Stop looking at what you don't have and start PRAISING HIM FOR THE GOOD THINGS YOU DO HAVE!!

Paul goes on to say this next:

Romans 11:36 ...everything exists by [Jesus'] power... (NLT)

What he is saying here is everything we care about holds together because of Christ's power, not ours.

Let's go back to our list:

Your marriage stays together not because you work on it, but because God allows it to stay together!

Your kids are not crazy not because you protect them well, but because God protects them well!

You have that job not because you work hard there, but because God allows you to keep working there by His grace!

Your home and car are not being paid for each month by you, but by Jesus and His grace. He allows you to keep your job, pay your mortgage, and keep your car accident-free.

Your talent will continue to get better and better not because of your hard work, but by His grace.

Your health is not because you eat right, but because He is blessing you today!

See, everything good in our lives is SUSTAINED, MAINTAINED, and HELD TOGETHER by Christ, not us! If this is the truth – TRUST HIM! Stop trying to keep everything together, and live by faith that He will keep it together!

Trust Him with your marriage, your kids, your finances, your career, your house payment, your car, your talents, and your health! He has not forgotten you. He will not abandon you! You are the righteousness of God in Christ Jesus! You are deeply loved, highly favored, greatly blessed, totally righteous, and destined to reign!

This is WHO YOU ARE! So trust Him! He will hold your life together!

But what happens when it looks like it's falling apart instead? What happens then? I need to say something to you about this. If He takes a gift from you, you must know He has something else for you!

Here is what I mean: If God allows you to lose your home, know that He has not abandoned you, but has a good plan for you post-house!

For example: A couple in our church was foreclosed upon. They were heartbroken. They had worked to keep that home for several years, and they still lost it. Two months later, they got a call from a relative in Europe offering them a job and a place to live. Now their family has the opportunity to go live abroad for a year! This would have never happened if they still had their mortgage here! They would have been tied down.

Sometimes God has to take something from you in order to give something to you! Now I know some of you are thinking: "But my spouse died or I lost my marriage. I don't want something else. I WANTED THEM!" As a pastor, I don't have an answer for you except to say: Trust Jesus. If He allowed them to be taken from you, know that God has good plans for you and for them as well!

He has something else for you! He has not abandoned you. You are His righteousness! He holds all things together by His power. If something has fallen apart, know He still has something good in your future! Your dream might have to change a little. Your plan might not be what you thought it would be. But know this: God will bring good things to pass in your life yet! Just stay in faith! Don't lose heart! Don't give up! You will see the goodness of the Lord!

Then Paul makes one last statement. This is the one that blows me away. If all He had made were the previous two statements, we could live self-centered lives and focus on our own enjoyment and success. But he makes a final statement that is so important:

Romans 11:36 ...is intended for [Jesus'] glory. (NLT)

In other words, every good gift in life from Jesus is given so that we will bring Jesus more fame in this world! The gifts God gives us are not just to use on ourselves or for our enjoyment, but ultimately to bring Jesus glory, fame, and honor!

He gave us our marriage so people would see Jesus in our love.

He gave us our finances so we would have resources to help others, and to bless the church and the world.

He gave us our health not to waste time on selfish pleasure, but to be used to serve others and Him.

He gave us our homes to house people in need and our cars to transport those who are without one.

EVERY GIFT WAS GIVEN SO THAT WE WOULD BRING JESUS FAME!

If this is the truth, maybe we could use everything we have for Him! Maybe we could serve Him!

We don't serve because we have to. We serve out of a deep understanding that everything is by His grace. We want to serve with our time, money, resources, and talents because God is so good to us!

Many Christians spend their lives serving their gifts rather than serving the Giver. Don't make an idol of your blessings! Don't make a god of the good things He gives you. Instead, use whatever good gifts He gives you to serve your good God!

He is the giver of all good things.

He is the sustainer of all good things.

He does this to bring more glory to Himself.

See, this world really isn't about us; it is about Jesus. It is always, only about Jesus.

CHAPTER 23

CONTAINERS OF GRACE

*"Amazing grace how sweet the sound
that saved a wretch like me."*
- John Newton

This is my last chapter, and I want to go back to our original idea. Grace freely flows from God. It is always an open bar that we never have to pay for. We just get to hold up our cup and drink freely from His grace!

So what we are, in effect, is containers of grace.

2 Corinthians 4:7 says we are like "common clay pots" or pitchers that collect living water!

We are designed to fill up on the grace of God.

We are designed to fill up on the favor of God.

We are designed to fill up on the blessings of God.

Then, when we are full – we spill grace on everyone around us. We spill favor on everyone around us. We spill blessing on everyone around us.

I want you to think about your life. Are you filled up with grace? Jesus was. (John 1:14) When you really come in contact with JESUS, the grace-filled one, you cannot help but get splashed by His grace.

This is what Christ wants for you. His heart is for you to come close to Him and let Him splash grace on you. He desires that **"streams of living water will flow from you." (John 7:38)** His heart is to fill you up, so that you can be poured out on others!

What I am trying to say is this:

You have just read a whole lotta pages about the grace of God. Have you let His grace truly fill you? The answer to that question can be found in these evidences:

The people around you are saying, "Wow! Something happened to you. You are different."

Your family says you smile more often.

Your friends see more joy in you.

Your enemies are noticing that you are not fighting back so much.

The people at work and school notice that you are freely, excitedly talking about your faith in Christ!

As you let grace fill you up, you will notice ALL your relationships are different. Mine are. I am not the same person I was a year ago. My friendships are different. My marriage is different. The way I parent is different. The way I lead our church is different. I knew I was on to something one day when Kelly (who I have been married to for almost eighteen years) looked at me and said, "I really like this new you!"

In that moment, I knew God's grace had done something in me that I could never do for myself. My life was radically changed when I realized God wanted me to live in His free grace and stop trying to pay for what He has covered.

I pray that you, too, have been radically transformed by His grace, and that you will splash it on others, spread the word that it's free, to the glory of Jesus.

AFTERTHOUGHT

A LETTER TO THE READER

Dear Reader,

This book is far from perfect, but hopefully it exalted the Perfect One. What I have tried to do in my finite way is express to you the INFINITE, radical, crazy, overwhelming, beautiful nature of grace.

I shared these words and thoughts with you because Jesus' grace compelled me to do so. I just can't keep quiet about what Christ did for me. I am so thankful for a "second work of grace" in my life, that I MUST share it.

Notice: I do not HAVE to share it. Jesus did not "should" me into writing it or dangle blessings in front of me if I would do it.

I wrote simply because I was compelled to write out of deep gratitude for the grace that Jesus has given me. I feel like He granted me a second season in life. A radically more abundant life than I could never have dreamed possible. I am overwhelmed by His grace available "on tap" for me.

I pray that in reading these pages Jesus' grace has overwhelmed you as well. I am hoping you shook, cried, prayed and praised like I did when I was struck so hardcore with the grace of Jesus a year ago.

But I am also praying that you would do more than just freak out and praise. I am hoping you are now compelled to share this radical grace with others.

I think about Saul's conversion to Paul on the Damascus Road. After meeting Jesus and His grace, Paul just could not keep silent about what The Lord had done for him. He spent the rest of His life explaining, exploring and expressing the greatness of grace!

I, too, have had a profound encounter with Christ and His grace, and I cannot keep silent about it. I've had to express it, and like Paul, I have faced ridicule, lies, false accusations and mocking because I cannot shut up about what I believe to be the truth of Grace.

I pray that this book has moved you to speak boldly about the Gospel of Grace with everyone you meet as well.

I pray that you cannot keep silent.

I pray that you tell your friends, family and co-workers of the greatness of His grace.

I pray that you overcome everything that the enemy throws at you in his quest to stop the Gospel of Grace.

I pray that multitudes of people meet Jesus because of your vocal, unwavering proclamation of grace to a world that desperately needs it.

Go in the grace and peace of our Lord Jesus Christ. Amen.

APPENDIX

THE TWELVE MILE MARKERS OF FREEDOM

Mile Marker # 1: We admit we are powerless over our hurt, habit, or hang-up and our lives are unmanageable.

Mile Marker # 2: We came to believe that Jesus and the power of His grace is the only thing that can restore me to sanity.

Mile Marker # 3: We turned our will and our lives over to the care of Jesus and His grace!

Mile Marker # 4: We examined ourselves and the root causes that led us to our hurt, habit, or hang-up.

Mile Marker # 5: We admit to ourselves, another, and Jesus the exact nature of our wrongs and throw ourselves into Christ's mercy and grace.

Mile Marker # 6: We became open for Jesus to remove our defects of character.

Mile Marker # 7: We believe that because of the cross and His grace, Jesus has forgiven us and freed us from our shortcomings.

Mile Marker # 8: Because of God's grace toward us, we became willing to seek forgiveness and restitution toward all people we have hurt.

Mile Marker # 9: Because of God's grace toward us, we sought forgiveness and restitution toward all the people we have hurt, expect where to do so would cause more harm than good.

Mile Marker # 10: We live life in Christ "by His grace"; therefore when we are wrong we promptly admit it to God and others.

Mile Marker # 11: We seek through daily prayer and the Word of God to better understand the depths of God's grace for us.

Mile Marker # 12: Having been set free by the grace of God, we seek to bring freedom and grace to others as well.

ABOUT ERIC DYKSTRA

Eric Dykstra is a former freaked-out Christian overachiever who is now resting in the grace of God found in the New Covenant. He and his wife Kelly founded The Crossing, a multi-site church north of Minneapolis. Eric's passions include seeing broken people far from God come to know the amazing grace of Jesus, fishing on the Rum River for smallmouth bass, and traveling with his family.

On the web, you can find Eric & Kelly's ministry in the following places:

PastorEricDykstra.com (Eric's blog)

KellyDykstra.com (Kelly's blog)

Twitter: @EricDykstra, @KellyDykstra

Their sermons may be found on www.Crossing-Church.com.

The Crossing (Crossing-Church.com) is based in Elk River, Minnesota, with campuses in surrounding towns. It is known widely for its unique approach to reaching those who feel the need for God's grace the most. The grace message and its accompanying Holy Spirit power is continually transforming the people of The Crossing.

The Crossing College (TheCrossingCollege.com) equips members of the Body of Christ to live out their calling.

Crossing Creative (CrossingCreative.com) leads The Crossing in worship and publishes original worship music. *Grace is Life* (GraceisLife.com) is their debut album, combining intentional, grace-centric lyrics with their signature rock & roll-style of worship. Available on iTunes and Amazon.

A small-group study guide for *Grace on Tap* is available. Please visit www.GraceOnTap.net for information.